The World's Metropolitan Areas

INTERNATIONAL URBAN RESEARCH
Institute of International Studies
University of California, Berkeley

The World's Metropolitan Areas

Berkeley and Los Angeles 1959
UNIVERSITY OF CALIFORNIA PRESS

*Members of the staff of
International Urban Research
who participated in this study:*

Suzanne R. Angelucci

Harley L. Browning

Kingsley Davis

Richard L. Forstall

Jack P. Gibbs

Gene B. Petersen

Thomas O. Wilkinson

Suggested citation for reference purposes:
International Urban Research, *The World's Metropolitan Areas*
(Berkeley and Los Angeles: University of California
Press, 1959)

UNIVERSITY OF CALIFORNIA PRESS
BERKELEY AND LOS ANGELES, CALIFORNIA

CAMBRIDGE UNIVERSITY PRESS
LONDON, ENGLAND

PREFACE

In 1956 the Ford Foundation granted the University of California the principal funds for a five-year research program on cities and urbanization throughout the world. With these funds the International Urban Research center was established on the Berkeley campus, under the aegis of the University's Institute of International Studies.

As a first step in the systematic collection and analysis of comparative urban statistics, the staff of IUR undertook to ascertain the number, location, size, components, and growth of metropolitan areas. Although other projects were begun at the same time, it was felt that this particular undertaking was basic to much later work. The available data on cities, although often used and cited, suffer from serious defects. Among these the most important is the lack of comparability from one country to another in the way cities are delimited. A second important defect is the lack of correspondence between cities, so-called, and the actual urban aggregates. The International Urban Research center therefore tried to establish greater international comparability in the delimitation of urban populations, and to do this in terms of a unit, the metropolitan area, which would embrace the actual urban aggregates.

The present monograph is the first result of this effort. It provides, for the benefit of urban scholars, a list of the world's metro-

[v]

politan areas of more than 100,000 inhabitants, classified by continent and country, showing the population of each area. It also provides a brief analysis of the problems of delimiting urban boundaries and a description of the procedures used by IUR in its own delimitations.

This task required detailed research on hundreds of urban places, the use of a variety of languages, and a search for scarce materials. The work has in every sense been a joint scientific enterprise of the IUR staff. Although the division of labor was primarily regional and linguistic, the discussion of techniques and problems benefited all.

Indispensable to the staff was the assistance of Mrs. Cleo C. Stoker, Administrative Assistant in the Institute of International Studies, Miss Clara C. Carroll, Secretary in the IUR office, Mrs. Doris Margolis and Miss Eleanor Langlois, Research Assistants. Richard Dempsey, who devoted an entire summer to the delimitation of metropolitan areas in England and Wales, deserves special recognition.

Appreciation is also due to the staff of the Library at the University of California in Berkeley, particularly the Documents Department, Interlibrary Borrowing Service, and the Map Collection. The persons in charge of these divisions have cheerfully and effectively tried to meet innumerable requests for materials. Libraries in other parts of the country, particularly the Stanford Library, have generously lent us books.

It is an especially pleasant duty to acknowledge the great aid received from abroad. Our sincere appreciation goes to the numerous officials and experts in foreign countries who have patiently read our letters and have responded by furnishing information that was not only necessary but in many cases not otherwise obtainable. These conscientious respondents included statistical and government officers in many countries and territories of the world, and also United States information officers and diplomatic staff members stationed abroad. We can only hope that our publications—the present one and those to come—will provide some advance in the understanding of urbanization and in this way repay the kindness of all those who helped us. We also hope that urban scholars throughout the world will find our publications useful, that some scholars will be able to come to Berkeley to take advantage of our accumulated files, and that we shall have the opportunity to provide laboratory training for foreign students of urbanization.

Of course, IUR alone assumes responsibility for the materials it presents in this document. Such responsibility is sobering, because the nature of the task is such that perfection cannot be achieved. This first effort to provide data on all metropolitan areas of the world is necessarily incomplete and tentative. We welcome criticism and hope that it will not only help us to correct errors but will also contribute to an increased interest in the problems of urban analysis and urban planning.

KINGSLEY DAVIS

University of California, Berkeley
December, 1958

CONTENTS

URBAN SCIENCE

AND COMPARATIVE ANALYSIS

During the last century and a half the world has experienced revolutionary developments greater than in all of its previous history combined. One of these developments is rapid and accelerating urbanization. Not only have towns and cities multiplied over the globe, but an ever greater proportion of the human population is living in these places.

Since an urban mode of life is fundamentally different from a rural one, and since the process of urbanization is related to other revolutionary developments in human society, research devoted to cities and to urbanization has increased during the past fifty years. Indeed, the study of urban phenomena has begun to take on the aspect of a formal scientific discipline, as implied in such terms as "urban sociology," "urban ecology," and "urban geography."

Scientific study in this field, however, has been hampered by the lack of systematic comparative analysis. Most investigations have been confined to particular cities or, at best, to particular countries. If there is to be a true science of urban phenomena, if a body of general explanatory and predictive principles is to be achieved, this particularism must be overcome.

The paucity of comparative urban research is of course not due to indifference or lack of foresight on the part of social scientists, but to the absence of comparable, or standardized, information from one country to another, and to the technical problems presented by this deficiency. The units of observation themselves—that is, "cities" and "towns"—have not been standardized, nor have we had information on a representative sample of these for the world as a whole. Most of our data have pertained to the "cities" of the West, although just as many "cities" are to be found in the rest of the world. Furthermore, the structure of urban communities has changed with increasing urbanization—a change that has gone further in some countries than in others. This dynamic element has meant that definitions of urban places adequate for one region or time have not been suitable for another region or time. Still another feature offering an obstacle to comparative analysis, is the complexity of urban centers. Since cities include virtually every aspect of human existence, they can be studied from many points of view, with the consequence that comparative analysis, if it were to be complete, would require the standardization of a bewildering variety of types of information.

Some of these problems have become less serious because our ability to separate the various aspects of cities for specialized analytical study has improved; and the output of basic statistical data from the various countries of the world has increased in recent years. These two developments are mutually reinforcing and stimulating. The greater sharpness of our conceptual tools enables us to separate the chaff from the grain, to ask specific questions about cities to which specific answers are possible. The improvement of the tools, however, would be halted if theories could not be tested with empirical data. Of course, the scope and reliability of information on urban communities are largely beyond the immediate control of the person engaged in comparative analysis; he must, for the most part, use whatever information governments see fit to gather and publish. But with more urban information available now than ever before, the greater effort of social scientists to utilize the data in censuses, vital statistics, special surveys, and field investigations, will itself result in the improvement of the sources. As the critical evaluation of basic data and the clarification of methodological issues take place, changes will surely be made in official procedures. This increasing opportunity for fruitful interaction between the prosecution of analytical research and the gathering of statistical information augurs well for the further development of urban studies.

One way to maximize the opportunity now existing is to push

ahead in the field of comparative study. Such an effort always runs into the criticism that international comparisons of urban phenomena are impossible, because the data are not yet sufficiently abundant nor sufficiently comparable. However, if we waited until complete information were available before attempting scientific inquiry, we would wait forever.

PURPOSE OF THE PRESENT STUDY

The goal of the research reported here is limited to the selection of one aspect of urban communities—their territorial extent and population. We have tried to approximate a standard "unit of observation," the Metropolitan Area[1] or M.A.—hoping to establish such units for each country and to give the number of their inhabitants.

This procedure represents a departure from the usual practice of gathering and presenting data on "cities." Such "cities" have usually been demarcated by purely political boundaries, with the consequence that their extent is arbitrary from a demographic and ecological point of view. Since ways of delimiting cities vary from country to country, depending upon the political and administrative peculiarities of each nation, the units thus presented are not even approximately standardized. This frequently leads to false conclusions on the part of those unfamiliar with these local distinctions. In 1957, for example, New York City had less than eight million inhabitants. In the same year Tokyo was estimated to have *more* than eight million. Press commentators drew the conclusion that New York is smaller than Tokyo. If this were true, it would be a puzzle why a nation nearly twice as large and more industrialized than Japan should have a smaller financial and business capital. The truth is, of course, that different entities were being compared. From a demographic and economic point of view, the boundaries of New York City do not describe a separate entity, nor do the political boundaries of Tokyo. The metropolitan area of New York contains more than fourteen million people, about three million more than the metropolitan area of Tokyo. New York, as an ecological entity, therefore, has a substantially larger population than Tokyo.

[1] Throughout this report the capitalization of the term "Metropolitan Area" or its abbreviation "M.A." refers specifically to IUR's version of the concept.

In an effort to avoid the arbitrariness of "cities" as urban units for statistical purposes, several countries have delimited larger units by one means or another. These units have been variously named—"urban agglomerations," "conurbations," "urbanized areas," or "metropolitan areas"—depending partly on the procedures followed in delimiting them. They have often been specifically identified by an adjective preceding the name of the principal political city, such as "Greater London," "Greater Tokyo," or "Metropolitan New York." These efforts have increased the international comparability of cities, but the countries in which such units have been designated are few, and the procedures followed have not been necessarily comparable.

IUR has followed the example of the few countries that delimit metropolitan areas.[2] Such areas are meant to include the territory surrounding a city if it represents a continuous extension of the city or if the people living there are predominantly connected with the city in an intimate day-to-day economic and occupational sense. The main contribution of the present monograph, therefore, is the delimitation of metropolitan areas throughout the world according to an approximately standardized method, and the provision of a table listing these areas, their principal cities, and their populations as of two recent dates. In addition, an appendix gives the sources of information and the component units used in the construction of each M.A.

We would have preferred to give more information about each M. A. than is presented in the table and the appendix. The square miles of land, the composition of the labor force, the age structure of the population—all would have been valuable. Unfortunately, however, an attempt to cover additional variables would have entailed another year or more of work. Rather than hold up the reporting of the population and component units for each M.A., we thought it preferable to publish the table now, hoping to supply additional information later.

It should be clear that the work reported here has not been merely a compilation of existing information. It has been rather a research project requiring the analysis of data for a purpose for which they were not originally meant. The results have been reached frequently only after the testing of different types of in-

---

[2] Australia, Canada, Japan, and Sweden are examples of countries that have made a special effort in this direction.

formation against the established criteria. Even the search for relevant information for analysis has been more like prospecting than compiling. Linguistic barriers had to be surmounted, and decisions have had to be made on the basis of the best judgment possible in the light of conflicting information.

This effort to increase the scope and comparability of materials available for international studies of urbanization has been faced with two methodological problems. The initial problem, as indicated, was to establish a unit of observation which promised a higher degree of standardization than those currently employed. The second problem was to identify and delimit the places that met the established criteria and thus qualified as M. A.'s. Beyond these two problems our goal was to report the number of inhabitants in each M.A. at different points in time, with a view to providing information on population growth.

For reasons explained below, neither of these problems could be perfectly solved. Even on a theoretical level, the metropolitan area is not the ideal unit. It is certainly the most feasible unit for comparative purposes; but, even so, the operational definition of metropolitan areas cannot be completely standardized, and in some countries it cannot be applied at all for lack of basic information.

URBAN AGGREGATES AND THEIR DELIMITATION

FOR INTERNATIONAL COMPARISON

Data on "cities" in census reports and other official or scholarly sources are frequently not comparable within the same country, much less between different countries.[3] The usual demarcation of a city is a political one which is often quite arbitrary from the standpoint of the actual pattern of settlement. The political limits may remain fixed while the urban population expands beyond, or the boundary may be arbitrarily extended to include areas that are essentially rural. Further, the extent and the direction of the discrepancy between political and ecological boundaries varies from one city to the next.

LOGICAL POSSIBILITIES OF DISCREPANCY

The relation between the "city" as officially defined and the "urban aggregate"[4] as ecologically conceived may take any one of the following forms:

I. *The Underbounded City: The "city" smaller than the urban aggregate.* The rest of the urban aggregate (the continuous urban territory) may be:

---

[3] For evidence of this see G. Goudswaard, "Quelques notes sur les concepts de 'ville' et 'agglomeration,' " *Proceedings of the World Population Conference, 1954* (New York: United Nations, 1955), IV, 685–693.

[4] The term urban aggregate is used here in a generic sense.

1) Left without any demarcation between it and surrounding administratively rural territory, or
2) Divided up among other "cities" and administratively rural territory.

II. *The Overbounded City: The "city" larger than the urban aggregate.* This "city" includes both urban and rural territory. The former may consist of:
1) Only one continuous urban aggregate.
2) More than one separate urban aggregate.

III. *The Truebounded City: The "city" virtually identical with the urban aggregate.* This is the ideal because the political and demographic-ecological boundaries correspond.

The first two types raise a question concerning the ratio between the urban and rural territory, and between the urban and rural population, within the larger boundary. In Type I, the area administratively defined as rural—that is, within the urban aggregate but outside any municipalities—may either exceed or be less than the territory within the municipality; the people who live within the urban aggregate but outside the municipality may either be more or less than the number living in the municipality. These possibilities exist even though the total aggregate in Type I comprises only urban territory and population. In other words, by definition the administrative city will not include rural territory, because it is smaller than the urban aggregate.

Type II has four possibilities: with respect to *territory* (a) the rural territory may exceed the urban territory, or (b) vice versa. With respect to *population* (a) the rural population may exceed the urban population, or (b) vice versa.

Both Type I and Type II are oversimplifications. Frequently the demographic-ecological boundary of a city crosses its administrative boundary at two or more points, thus creating a mixture of Types I and II, which will not be considered here.

To illustrate our typology, let us consider the kinds of municipal units found in three contrasting countries. In Pakistan the boundaries of the officially defined city often correspond closely to the continuous urban area. Pakistani cities thus approach the ideal, Type III. In Australia, large continuous urban areas tend to be divided politically into municipalities, municipal corporations, cities, towns, boroughs, shires, and district councils; and Adelaide, Melbourne, Perth, and Sydney proper had populations of

[7]

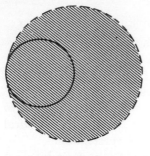

I. 1   I. 2

Type I. **The Underbounded City**
    ("City" smaller than the urban aggregate).

II. 1   II. 2

Type II. **The Overbounded City**
    ("City" larger than the urban aggregate).

Legend. "City" boundaries, principal city, shown in solid line. "City" boundaries, subsidiary cities, shown in dotted line. "Urban aggregate" boundaries shown in broken line; shading within these indicates urban settlement.

less than 100,000 in 1947.[5] Australian cities thus resemble Type I.2. In the Philippines the political boundaries of most "cities" include huge areas of land that admittedly are distinctly rural, along with towns of various sizes.[6] This corresponds to Type II.2.

ALTERNATIVE PATHS TO COMPARABILITY

Since most political cities are either Type I or Type II or a mixture of the two, the student of comparative urbanization must either find some way of eliminating the discrepancy between the "city" and the urban aggregate, or he must redefine the unit of observation in such a way as to make the degree and direction of the discrepancy roughly comparable from case to case and from country to country. The first alternative calls for the delimitation of the urbanized area, the territory settled continuously in an urban fashion; the second for the delimitation of some other area —the metropolitan area—which includes not only all or most of the continuous urban territory but usually some rural territory as well.[7]

Whereas the boundaries of urban units within the same country are often at least drawn within the framework of a common political institution, there is no necessity for different countries to follow a common procedure in drawing such boundaries. In most countries the fact that the political boundaries are not keeping pace with the growth of urban settlement (Type I) makes the political city a questionable unit of observation, but the other source of error (Type II) is more frequent than generally realized.

---

[5] The situation in Australia is made less complicated by the fact that the population of metropolitan divisions which encompass the larger continuous urban areas are given in Australian census reports. However, these official metropolitan areas are not necessarily comparable with those delimited by other countries or by IUR.

[6] This accounts for the exclusion of the "chartered cities" of Bacolod, Basilan, Davao, and Zamboanga from the list of M.A.'s in the Philippines. These four "cities," which had a population of more than 100,000 each in 1948, may be characterized as highly "overbounded."

[7] The discrepancy between the areal size of the metropolitan area and that of the urbanized area is admittedly not a desirable situation. However, for our purposes not the areal extent but the number of people is primarily important. Thus, if 90 per cent of the population of a metropolitan area is within the urbanized area, the fact that the metropolitan area may be much larger in extent than the urbanized area is of secondary importance.

[9]

In the few countries where the entire zones of continuous urban settlement for each urban center have been demarcated, political lines, especially the municipal boundaries of the "city" proper, have necessarily been abandoned. The statistical limits must remain flexible, for as the urban population spreads into new territory, the dimensions of the continuous urban area necessarily change.

The United States is one of the countries that have attempted to delimit actual urbanized areas. It initiated this policy for the 1950 census. The following account describes the procedure used.[8]

An urbanized area is an area that includes at least one city with 50,000 inhabitants or more in 1940 or later according to a special census taken prior to 1950 and also the surrounding closely settled incorporated places and unincorporated areas that meet the criteria listed below. Since the urbanized area outside of incorporated places was defined on the basis of housing or population density or of land use, its boundaries for the most part are not political but follow such features as roads, streets, railroads, streams, and other clearly defined lines which may be easily identified by census enumerators in the field. The urbanized area boundaries were selected after careful examination of all available maps, aerial photographs, and other sources of information, and then were checked in detail in the field by trained investigators to insure that the criteria were followed and that the boundaries were identifiable.

The delineation of the boundaries of the urbanized areas had to be completed prior to the beginning of enumeration; consequently, it was not possible to establish urbanized areas in connection with those cities which attained a population of 50,000 or more according to the 1950 Census. Urbanized areas were established for Fort Smith, Ark., and Muskegon, Mich., both of which had in excess of 50,000 inhabitants according to special censuses

[8] U. S. Bureau of the Census, *U. S. Census of Population: 1950*, "United States Summary" (Washington: United States Government Printing Office, 1953), II, Part I, 21–22.

conducted prior to 1950. The population of both of these cities fell below 50,000 in 1950. The urbanized areas defined for these two cities, however, were retained in the tabulations.

The urban fringe of an urbanized area is that part which is outside the central city or cities. The following types of areas are embraced if they are contiguous to the central city or cities or if they are contiguous to any area already included in the urban fringe:

1. Incorporated places with 2,500 inhabitants or more in 1940 or at a subsequent special census conducted prior to 1950.

2. Incorporated places with fewer than 2,500 inhabitants containing an area with a concentration of 100 dwelling units or more with a density in this concentration of 500 units or more per square mile. This density represents approximately 2,000 persons per square mile and normally is the minimum found associated with a closely spaced street pattern.

3. Unincorporated territory with at least 500 dwelling units per square mile.

4. Territory devoted to commercial, industrial, transportational, recreational, and other purposes functionally related to the central city.

Also included are outlying noncontiguous areas with the required dwelling unit density located within $1\frac{1}{2}$ miles of the main contiguous urbanized part, measured along the shortest connecting highway, and other outlying areas within one-half mile of such noncontiguous areas which meet the minimum residential density rule.

A somewhat similar delimitation, though by different methods, has been attempted in England and Wales. Instead of the term "urbanized areas," the units thus demarcated in the English census go under the name of "conurbations."[9] Geddes's characterization of a conurbation has been quoted by the Registrar-General in an official publication as follows:

[9] Some European writers are prone to identify conurbations with Standard Metropolitan Areas rather than Urbanized Areas.

... an area occupied by a continuous series of dwellings, factories and other buildings, harbour and docks, urban parks and playing fields, etc., which are not separated from each other by rural land; though in many cases in this country such an urban area includes enclosures of rural land which is still in agricultural occupation.[10]

The Registrar-General quotes the Geddes definition with approval except to say that it was perhaps too much concerned with bricks and mortar and too little with the interrelation of the center and the periphery through commuting and daily contact. However, when the Registrar-General states the procedural criteria used in delimiting conurbations in England and Wales, he seems to have envisaged metropolitan areas:

. . . each conurbation should be an aggregate of local authority areas. Three other factors of varying importance were also to be taken into account; first, that the conurbation generally should be a continuously built-up area, but on the one hand this should not include ribbon development, and on the other it should not necessarily exclude a built-up area separated by a narrow strip of rural land from the main built-up area to which it was strongly attached for employment or other reasons; second, that a local area should be considered for inclusion in a conurbation to whose focal centre it was strongly attached as a centre for work, shopping, higher education, sports or entertainment; third, that some consideration should be given to population density.[11]

What makes this resemble the definition of a metropolitan area is the decision to use entire administrative areas as constituents. However, since the areas used are generally small, the resulting conurbation more closely resembles an urbanized area than it does a metropolitan area.

Sometimes countries present data on urbanized areas without specifying clearly how the areas were delimited. The main compilation of data is provided by the Statistical Office of the United Nations. In its *Demographic Yearbook* for 1957 the populations of

---

[10] General Register Office, *Census, 1951, England and Wales,* "Report on Greater London and Five Other Conurbations" (London: H.M.S.O., 1956), p. xiv.

[11] *Ibid.,* p. xv.

one or more "urban agglomerations" in 44 countries or territories are reported. Apart from the fact that many countries and territories are not included, the table giving the figures (Table 5) is reduced in value by the lack of comparability. For most countries or territories only a few urban agglomerations are shown. Further, as noted by the Statistical Office, the way in which the urban agglomerations were delimited varies from one country to another; and, although the component units are sometimes given in the footnotes, the criteria used for establishing the limits of each agglomeration are not stated. Probably many of these agglomerations fit the concept of the metropolitan area better than they fit the concept of the urbanized area. The Statistical Office had to rely for the most part on the population figures and units of observation defined by each country. Its hands were thus tied in attempting to establish comparability.

Although the concept of the urbanized area, by whatever name, is theoretically the best for describing and understanding urban communities, it suffers from several difficulties that stand in the way of its use for international comparison. In the first place, the essence of this idea is that, in the demarcation of the area, political boundaries are either to be ignored or to be given second place. Since the boundary is to depend on the actual pattern of settlement at the moment rather than upon any fixed line, the delimitation must be done at the time, or just before, the data are gathered, often by field representatives on the spot. Consequently, if a country does not report statistics for such urbanized areas, it is difficult for an investigator coming later, who must depend upon reported data, to delimit these. In other words, the boundaries of urbanized areas should ideally be decided upon when the census office is mapping the country for the purpose of enumerating the population. Persons having their residence inside the urbanized areas can thus be distinguished, when the enumeration is completed, from those residing outside. If a government has not followed such procedures, the researcher cannot assemble relevant data on urbanized areas. The only solution to the problem would come if all governments demarcated urbanized areas according to a standard procedure and prepared reports on the populations and other statistical aspects of these areas.

Most governments do not, and hardly will in the future, delimit true urbanized areas. The reason for this points to the second difficulty in the application of the concept—namely, since the boundaries of each urbanized area generally must be changed from one census to the next, they cannot correspond to the territorial limits of local civil divisions. Boundaries of urbanized areas tend to cut across established and fixed administrative lines which are known to the people and related to well-known political divisions in the territorial organization of the nation. It follows that not only does a government face an extra task of mapping and tabulating when it tries to delimit urbanized areas, but it has no easy way of relating the census data on such areas to the varied types of data available for established local territorial units. Ordinarily local statistics are gathered under local authorities operating in fixed local territories. Hence the registration figures for births, deaths, marriages, divorces, employment, school enrollment, and so on cannot easily be related to census data on urbanized areas. One might say that the urbanized area suffers the defect of its great virtue. Since its boundaries change from year to year, it can keep up with the expansion of the urban population; but it is by that very fact not an administrative unit and hence is not controlled as a unit by agencies registering vital events. This is due in part to the fact that the boundaries of urbanized areas are not known by the public, who therefore cannot say whether they live in or out of the area when they give information to a registrar. In view of the difficulty of relating noncensus data to the census data for urbanized areas, the value of the latter is greatly lessened; essential types of statistical analysis, such as the computation of birth and death rates, are either precluded or made difficult for the urbanized areas. In view of this defect, governments are not likely to engage in the task of providing data on urbanized areas.

If the investigator wishes to use urbanized areas as his units of observation, he must usually construct them himself from such data on politically defined units as he can find. If, for example, he can obtain statistical information on very small units such as precincts, census tracts, farms, villages, and towns, he can often combine these in such a way as to approximate the urbanized areas. The work involved in this procedure, however, generally will lie beyond the resources of any private project. Furthermore, for many countries it is impossible to find the requisite data, especially since in constructing the urbanized areas the investigator must have not only the population of the small areas he is combining but also other data such as geographical area, population characteristics, and types of land use.

The Delimitation of Metropolitan Areas

The other alternative is to give up the idea of using urbanized areas for international comparison in favor of another concept which, though theoretically less desirable, is practically more feasible. This other concept, the metropolitan area, accepts the fact of political boundaries but tries to use them in such a way as to include the continuous urban area. Instead of taking the boundaries of the corporate city as defining an ecological unit, it pays attention to territorial units beyond the corporate city, seeking to find boundaries that include the actual urban area but do not include preponderantly rural territory. In this way, a rough comparability from one region or country to another can be achieved. The error tends to run usually in the same direction—that is, toward including more area and more people than the actual urbanized area comprises. This at once reduces much of the variation that would be encountered if "cities" per se were used as the units, and it has the further advantage that the rural areas included are apt to be the ones into which the urban population is destined soon to expand. This in turn suggests that metropolitan areas, in comparison to urbanized areas, are more stable units and, as a consequence, more useful for historical comparisons. It should also be noted that, unlike the urbanized area, the components of an operationally defined metropolitan area are administrative units, and whatever statistical data are available for these units can be used to study the metropolitan area as a whole or its internal structure.

OTHER IDEAS AND APPROACHES

We have been addressing ourselves to the problem of demarcating urban units. We think of a "city," in the common acceptance of the term, as a relatively small area in which a large number of people are concentrated at a density much greater than that outside the area. Thus our preference would be to speak in terms of urbanized areas if this were possible; as this is impossible on an international basis, we have chosen the next best unit for standardization, the metropolitan area.

Since, however, our ultimate purpose is to understand the structure, distribution, and growth of cities, and to ascertain the causes and consequences of urbanization, we wish an approximation to the actual city in a demographic and ecological sense as our unit. Had our purpose been different, we might have sought another kind of unit. If, for example, the relation of the city to its hinterland had been our primary interest, we would have dealt with metropolitan regions, sometimes called "metropolitan communities."[12] These in each country would have embraced the entire national territory, whereas the metropolitan areas we have in mind do not divide up a whole country but are separated by territory that lies outside any metropolitan area.

Other terms—"megalopolis," "polynucleation," "urban complex"—are seldom used in an exact sense, but they seem to imply that the urban populations referred to are large and, therefore, spread out over a considerable territory. In this sense the terms are synonymous with very large city, or metropolis. In addition, however, an "urban complex" implies that several big cities have been combined into one, or may be imagined as so combined, because they have all spread out until they have become contiguous; or, at the least, the term implies that the urban aggregate is multi-nucleated.[13] Doubtless such terms could be used to designate some of the M. A.'s in our list. However, vague concepts of this sort are sometimes stretched to include much more. For instance, it has been said that Boston, New York, and Washington, D. C. are parts of one giant urban complex. Our interest in the present study does not lie in the analysis of the different forms in which cities can be grouped or related to the national economy, but in the demarcation of the areas of continuous and close urban settlement.[14]

A city is naturally thought about on two levels at once. On the

[12] See, for example, R. D. McKenzie, *The Metropolitan Community* (New York: McGraw-Hill, 1933), Parts 1–3; and Donald J. Bogue, *The Structure of the Metropolitan Community* (Ann Arbor: University of Michigan, 1949).

[13] These connotations have also come to be attached to the concept of conurbation.

[14] Some of the delimited M.A.'s show characteristics of multinucleation. An outstanding example is the Ruhr district. The cities of the "Inner Ruhr," however, have been separated from a greater region which is considered by many scholars to form an economically and socially integrated unit with

one hand, it is visualized as a place where a large number of people live together at a relatively high density. This would exclude 80,000 people in a football stadium, because, though densely packed, they do not *live* there; it would also exclude a village of, say, 800 people all living on six acres. Thus we think of Indianapolis and Ibadan as cities because several hundred thousand people live there together at an average density of thousands per square mile. On the other hand, we think of a city as a place where there are specialized occupations, an urban atmosphere, brisk trade, and bright lights. On this basis Indianapolis would certainly be included as a city, but some might exclude Ibadan (at least as it was two or three decades ago).

These two ways of looking at cities need not give rise to controversy. To view cities demographically is not to declare that they cannot be viewed politically or sociologically. The discrepancy between the political and the demographic city has political implications that the political scientist is best equipped to understand. The linkage between the parts of a metropolitan area, furthermore, is so much a matter of economics that we have used certain economic criteria in judging whether to include or exclude certain districts.

THE "STANDARD METROPOLITAN AREA" AS DEVELOPED BY THE UNITED STATES CENSUS BUREAU

In the United States an effort has long been made by the Bureau of the Census (in conjunction with other interested agencies) to delimit urban aggregates that are larger than the political city proper and hence more relevant to demographic and economic analysis. Starting with the idea of the "metropolitan district" in 1910 (retrojected to 1900), the Bureau has gradually expanded the number of such areas and altered the definitions and criteria (and even the names) as conditions have changed. The latest units—those of 1950—include, in addition to cities proper, both the "Urbanized Area" and the "Standard Metropolitan Area."[15]

Cologne as its commercial center. A larger area in the Ruhr can be easily reconstructed from the M.A.'s listed separately in the table. Another example of the same kind is the Rand area of South Africa.

[15] The common abbreviation used for this long name is S.M.A. Throughout the present report, this abbreviation will be used when referring to the United States concept.

Since we have taken the Standard Metropolitan Area as a point of departure, the Census Bureau definition is presented here in detail:

Except in New England, a standard metropolitan area is a county or group of contiguous counties which contains at least one city of 50,000 inhabitants or more. In addition to the county, or counties, containing such a city, or cities, contiguous counties are included in a standard metropolitan area if according to certain criteria they are essentially metropolitan in character and socially and economically integrated with the central city.

The criteria of metropolitan character relate primarily to the character of the county as a place of work or as a home for concentrations of nonagricultural workers and their dependents. Specifically, these criteria are:

1. The county must (a) contain 10,000 nonagricultural workers, or (b) contain 10 percent of the nonagricultural workers working in the standard metropolitan area, or (c) have at least one-half of its population residing in minor civil divisions with a population density of 150 or more per square mile and contiguous to the central city.

2. Nonagricultural workers must constitute at least two-thirds of the total number of employed persons of the county.

The criteria of integration relate primarily to the extent of economic and social communication between the outlying counties and the central county as indicated by such items as the following:

1. Fifteen percent or more of the workers residing in the contiguous county work in the county containing the largest city in the standard metropolitan area, or

2. Twenty-five percent or more of the persons working in the contiguous county reside in the county containing the largest city in the standard metropolitan area, or

3. The number of telephone calls per month to the county containing the largest city of the standard metropolitan area from the contiguous county is four

or more times the number of subscribers in the contiguous county.

In New England, the city and town are administratively more important than the county, and data are compiled locally for such minor civil divisions. Here towns and cities were the units used in defining standard metropolitan areas, and most of the criteria set forth above could not be applied. In their place, a population density criterion of 150 persons or more per square mile, or 100 persons or more per square mile where strong integration was evident, has been used.[16]

Except in New England, the S. M. A.'s are made up of counties, because in the United States the county is generally the next largest major political unit after the city. Furthermore, except in New England, it is an important statistical unit. Many kinds of census and registration statistics are available by counties, so that, once the S.M.A.'s are determined, an abundance of data can be assembled for each S.M.A. by bringing together the statistics on the component counties. In this regard, the S.M.A.'s differ from the Urbanized Areas, for which, as we have seen, other economic, political, or demographic data cannot ordinarily be assembled.

It should be noted that each S.M.A. must have a "central city" (a political city) of not less than 50,000 inhabitants. The Bureau of the Census started with the idea of a city with political boundaries. As this concept proved inadequate from a demographic and economic point of view, the tendency was to adopt a unit that included contiguous areas into which the city's population had expanded. The "central city" remained the starting point, and its size determined whether the entire area was to be designated an S.M.A. Logically, one might think that the important criterion for setting up an S.M.A. is the size of the whole population of the prospective counties to be included, but the historical focus has been on the "central city."

Behind the idea of the "central city" is the notion that an urban aggregate has a nucleus—a nerve center, the dominant,

[16] U. S. Bureau of the Census, *op. cit.*, pp. 27–28. Some minor changes have recently been made in the criteria for defining S.M.A.'s. See Office of Statistical Standards, *Criteria for Defining Standard Metropolitan Areas* (Washington, D.C.: March, 1958).

or the most urbanized section. Obviously, not the whole of the largest city in the S.M.A. is such a nerve center, but the assumption seems to be that it at least contains the nerve center for the entire aggregate. This is why the largest city is called the "principal central" city. In the New York S.M.A., for example, the principal central city is New York rather than Newark or Jersey City. An S.M.A. may, of course, contain several political cities, as well as land that is not contained in any incorporated place.

Given a central city of the requisite size, the question then becomes which counties to include with it. Obviously, the county containing the central city must be included (one might call this the "central county" when other counties are also included). Any others must meet certain requirements to be included: they must be contiguous to the county containing the central city; they must manifest certain economic or demographic traits associated with urban residence in America; and they must show close connections with the central county. In sum, the S.M.A. is an operational concept by which urban aggregates can be roughly approximated in terms of local political units (counties) larger than politically defined cities.

MODIFICATIONS OF THE S.M.A. CONCEPT
FOR INTERNATIONAL COMPARISON

For various theoretical and practical reasons the United States specifications for the Standard Metropolitan Area could not be adopted for international application without modification. The criteria set up by the Bureau of the Census are, for the most part, adapted to conditions in the United States— conditions that do not entirely apply in the rest of the world. The S.M.A. concept was therefore used as a general model for our international unit, but specific criteria were altered.

Theoretical Reasons for Modification

The application of the criteria defining the S.M.A. does not result in the delimitation of metropolitan areas of perfect comparability even in the United States, the country for which the concept was designed, because the S.M.A., as mentioned above, does not escape the problem of political boundaries. It simply substitutes the county for the city in determining the outer limits of the urban aggregate;[17] the county is as much a political unit as the corporate city, and like other political units its boundaries are arbitrary and somewhat inflexible.

> The county is by no means a uniform unit of land area. In fact, there is an inverse relationship, on a state-by-state basis, between average size of county and population density. Hence, S.M.A.'s tend to be made up of rather gross area units in regions of low population density and rather fine units in regions of high density.[18]

The use of counties as units can result in the inclusion of areas that are not urbanized in any sense of the term. In some isolated cases, such as San Bernardino County in California, large strips of territory that are virtually uninhabited are included in an S.M.A. On the other hand, a small area that is distinctly metropolitan and certainly a part of the actual urban aggregate is sometimes excluded from the S.M.A. because the county of which it forms a minor part is predominantly agricultural.

An additional source of noncomparability is the dependence on corporate cities of 50,000 or more as the nucleus, or starting point, in the S.M.A. delimitation. Since the boundaries of these cities are legal rather than demographic, their use introduces an arbitrary element. If, for instance, the central city happens to have a small area and, because of this, falls below the 50,000 mark, the urban aggregate of which it is a part will not be defined as an S.M.A. regardless of the size of the total aggregate.

We have seen, however, that the use of counties and corporate cities as the units for constructing S.M.A.'s in the United States has the advantage of making available a rich assemblage of statistical data. This makes it possible to supply more information on S.M.A.'s than is possible with Urbanized Areas. Although the Urbanized Areas are doubtless more comparable across the nation, the advantage of the S.M.A. in terms of the multiple statistics

---

[17] Except in New England where cities and townships are used. In an effort to secure greater comparability, Bogue has delimited S.M.A.'s in New England on the basis of counties. See his *Population Growth in Standard Metropolitan Areas: 1900–1950* (Washington, D.C.: Housing and Home Finance Agency, 1953).

[18] Otis D. Duncan, "Research on Metropolitan Population: Evaluation of Data," *Journal of the American Statistical Association*, LI (December, 1956), 591–596.

available for such units outweighs the disadvantages of noncomparability. As a consequence, it appears that in the United States the S.M.A. is more useful than the Urbanized Area.

Practical Reasons for Modification

One immediate obstacle to the use of the S.M.A. concept in international analysis is the uniqueness of the county as an administrative and political entity. Countries outside the English tradition do not have units with precisely this structure, although many do have areal divisions of similar size and similar intermediate status. Accordingly, to apply the criteria of the S.M.A. internationally, county equivalents in each nation must be established. This can best be done by thinking of the county as the administrative district immediately larger than the corporate city and generally surrounding it.

However, certain countries do not have county equivalents in this sense. In some, the "cities" are surrounded by a large number of small administrative units, often smaller than the "city" itself. Even in the United States not all corporate cities are surrounded by or contained in one county, but the county is almost invariably the larger territorial unit and is intermediate between the city and the state. In certain other countries the only political division that completely surrounds the city is more the equivalent of a state or province, which may contain several independent and widely separated cities. The larger unit is then too big to serve as an inclusive unit for delimiting the metropolitan area.

Also, some governments do not attempt to separate the urban aggregate, or a part of it, from its environs. As a result, it is impossible to find an exact parallel to the "central city" component of the American S.M.A. In certain countries, for example, the control of the urban aggregate is simply merged in the government of some much wider unit. Thus in Latin America the *municipio* is characteristically the local governmental unit, and the urban centers within the *municipio* do not have a formal position in the political structure.[19] In this situation it is sometimes necessary to employ, as the nearest equivalent to the central city, a local

---

[19] The same is true for Italy and Spain, where urban aggregates are not defined politically. Here the nearest demographic equivalent to a central city is the urban aggregate which contains the town hall.

[22]

political entity that does not really fit the United States definition, or to abandon altogether the search for a political nucleus and take instead an urban center as a physical entity.

A further consideration is the varying stage of economic development in the different countries. Such variation is bound to reduce the comparability of specific criteria for metropolitan delimitation. For instance, in the United States the city is thought of as spreading its inhabitants and influence into the surrounding area, which led to the rule that a county must contain a corporate city of 50,000 or more people before it qualifies as an S.M.A. Such a limit would not necessarily be realistic for less developed countries. The fact that the United States is a highly industrialized and wealthy country enables its urban population to spread its residences into low-density suburbs. Therefore, even a small corporate city may be the center of a large metropolitan area which is predominantly urban and economically closely integrated. Hence the influence of a city's population size on its environs varies with the technological level of the society. In technologically advanced societies the territory surrounding corporate cities of only modest population size can be expected to have a metropolitan character, whereas in less advanced societies the central cities must be of considerable size before their environs take on this character. If this is true, the rule that as few as 50,000 inhabitants will qualify a "city" to be the nucleus of an S.M.A. may set the minimum too low for purposes of international comparison. The mechanical application of such a rule in the less developed countries might lead to the designation of county-equivalent territories as metropolitan areas when in fact they were distinctly nonmetropolitan. Even in the United States the automatic inclusion of the county containing the central city leads to an appreciable number of rural inhabitants being included in the population of many S.M.A.'s. Such an error would be much greater if the S.M.A. criteria were applied in all other countries.

There is another problem created by differences in economic development. The Bureau of the Census judges a contiguous county to be part of an S.M.A. if at least 15 per cent of its resident workers go to the central county to work, if at least 25 per cent of its total labor force resides in that county, or if its telephone calls to that area exceed the number of its own subscribers by at least four times. Such stipulations cannot be applied in most countries of the world because the requisite data are usually unobtainable and because the stipulations are not necessarily appropriate. Few countries provide statistical information on place of work and place of residence in a form suitable for use in delimiting metropolitan areas. As to telephone calls, we found no country where the information was available in suitable form. Even in the United States the data on place of work and on telephone calls are not readily available. To get this information the Bureau of the Census relied heavily on data which do not regularly appear in official publications. Special compilations of data were also necessary in Japan, where the Bureau of Statistics[20] has delimited metropolitan areas on the basis of criteria similar to those set up by the Bureau of the Census.

Even if the information were available, however, it would probably not have the same significance for metropolitan delimitation that it does in the United States. In countries with little large-scale industry but with much handicraft production, the separation of work place from residence has not gone nearly so far as it has in industrial countries, and the telephone is a less common instrument of communication. In the United States the criterion of telephone calls reflects an advanced technological culture and a national idiosyncrasy, and it could hardly be applied in similar fashion in other countries. Although statistics on commuting are pertinent to the delimitation of metropolitan areas, a low level of commuting from an area contiguous to the city is not conclusive evidence that the area lacks an urban character or that it fails to form part of the metropolitan system. In short, the three criteria pertaining to economic and social communication are too relative to conditions in the United States—conditions which represent an extreme case in the total array of countries—to be used in demarcating metropolitan areas on a global basis. In modified form, whenever the data can be obtained, they have some utility, not so much in determining whether an area adjacent to the city is "urban" or "rural," as in judging whether it is actually linked with the central city.

A final indication of the necessity of modifying the S.M.A. criteria for international application is the fact that the Bureau

---

[20] Japan, Prime Minister's Office, Statistics Bureau, *Nihon Hyojun Toshi Chizu Bunrui* (Japanese Standard Metropolitan Classification), March, 1954.

of the Census itself, in delimiting the S.M.A.'s, did not follow its criteria rigorously or mechanically. According to an official[21] of the Bureau of the Census, numerous decisions took into account factors not explicitly incorporated in the formal statement of the criteria; sometimes the data called for by the criteria were not available, and a decision had to be made on the basis of whatever information was on hand. Also, local opinion regarding the applicability of the S.M.A. criteria was considered. How much influence such ad hoc decisions had on the actual delimitation of S.M.A.'s in 1950 is hard to say, but if modifications of this sort were required in the United States itself, one can see that a realistic adaptation of the criteria for world-wide application must use factors not included in the United States definition.

PROCEDURE FOR DELIMITING METROPOLITAN AREAS

The definition of Metropolitan Area (M.A.) adopted in this project for purposes of international comparison is as follows:

> An area with 100,000 or more inhabitants, containing at least one city (or continuous urban area) with 50,000 or more inhabitants and those administrative divisions contiguous to the city (or to the continuous urban area) which meet certain requirements as to metropolitan character.

Each element in this definition calls for comments.

The Principal City, or Urban Nucleus

As in the American S.M.A., the demarcation of an M.A. for our purposes starts with a "city" of 50,000 or more inhabitants.[22] Since, however, as explained earlier, the boundaries of a city are defined in different ways in different countries, and sometimes not defined at all, we have to allow for a reasonable specification of the urban nucleus when the official data do not come in precisely that form. For this reason, the main continuous

---

[21] Henry S. Shryock, Jr., "The Natural History of Standard Metropolitan Areas," *American Journal of Sociology*, LXIII (September, 1957), 163–170.

[22] All population limits incorporated in the criteria refer to population size as of the year of the census on which the delimitation is based. This is almost always the last census year before 1954.

urban area may be taken as the principal city even when it has no separate political structure or when the political "city" is clearly unrealistic or aberrant from a demographic and ecological point of view.[23]

In other words, we treat as a continuous urban area, and hence as a principal city, two or more "cities" that are physically adjacent. We also treat any administrative unit employed in a census report as a continuous urban area, and hence as a principal city, if it actually has this character, even though it lacks the political functions generally ascribed to a corporate city. In essence, this means that when the occasion calls for it and when census data are available for areal units, we can take a physical equivalent of a city as the nucleus for an M.A., despite the absence of any political entity corresponding to this equivalent. This device is adopted for those countries where the political boundaries of "cities" have little or no correspondence to what is physically an urban community, or where cities have no status as local government areas. Fortunately, such cases are comparatively rare. In some instances, in order to do as little violence as possible to the local definitions, we have modified our rule and dipped below the 50,000 minimum for the central nucleus. Thus, in Australia, the municipal corporation of Adelaide was treated as the principal city of Adelaide M.A. even though its 1947 population was below 50,000, the municipal corporation being only a part of a much larger continuous urban area with a population of well over 50,000. A similar situation is found in Malta, where Valletta, the capital, with a population of only 18,666, was taken as the principal city of an M.A. Charleroi in Belgium is another example of a principal city of less than 50,000. Like Adelaide, the municipalities of both Valletta and Charleroi are only parts of larger continuous urban areas.

The 100,000 Minimum for the Metropolitan Area

The table of M.A.'s throughout the world includes only those units that have a total of 100,000 or more inhabitants. The United States S.M.A. has no such lower limit, but we felt that this mini-

---

[23] Because of the frequent absence of data on the demographic and ecological characteristics of areal units within the city, we often found it necessary to accept the political boundary of the city as approximating an urban nucleus.

mum figure was satisfactory for our purposes. A minimum for the total M.A. clearly eliminates some urban areas that have a central nucleus of more than 50,000 inhabitants, but it does allow for the inclusion of central cities with that number when they are parts of an area which is metropolitan in character and has more than 100,000 inhabitants.

Contiguous Areas

In formulating the criteria for the inclusion of administrative divisions contiguous to the principal city (or to the continuous urban area), we found it impossible, for reasons stated above, to employ those parts of the S.M.A. criteria which relate to place of work or to telephone calls. Actually, for England and Wales, where the data were available from the 1951 census, we did use place-of-work data in the demarcation of M.A.'s in much the same way as they are used in the United States for the S.M.A.'s. In Scotland, Austria, Switzerland, Germany, and the Netherlands such data served only as a guide to M.A. delimitations.

The only S.M.A. criterion that offered the promise of world-wide application was the stipulation that nonagricultural workers constitute at least two-thirds of the total number of employed persons in the county. In accepting this part of the S.M.A. procedure, we modified it slightly to read as follows: Any administrative division which is considered a county equivalent must have, to be included in an M.A., at least 65 per cent of its labor force working in economic activities other than agriculture (which is meant here to include hunting and fishing as well as farming). Necessarily, such a division had also to include or be contiguous to the principal city (or urban nucleus) or to touch upon an administrative division already included in the M.A.

Clearly, by this rule, administrative divisions that surround or touch upon the principal city are *not automatically* included in the M.A. Equally apparent is the possibility that, as in some S.M.A.'s in the United States, several rings of administrative divisions lying around the principal city may be included, because a division that meets the nonagricultural requirement need only touch upon a division already included in the M.A.

Two types of exceptions to the nonagricultural rule were allowed. First, an administrative division not meeting the requirement was *included* in the M.A. if it was completely surrounded by administrative divisions that did meet it and which were themselves included. Second, an administrative division actually meeting the nonagricultural requirement was *excluded* if it was too far from the principal city. Although an M.A. can consist of several rings of administrative divisions around a city, each division, even though it meets the nonagricultural rule, must be close enough to the city to make feasible direct participation in the city's economic life. No hard and fast rule could be laid down as to exactly how close an administrative division had to be to the principal city to be included in the M.A. Each case had to be judged in relative terms, with attention given to the efficiency of the local transportation system, the existence of physical barriers, and the location of transport and other facilities. If distance had not been taken into account in some way, we would in some cases have faced the possibility of enormously extended "metropolitan areas." Thus in England a large part of the country might have formed a single metropolitan area.

When an administrative division was located close to the midpoint *between* two principal cities and could conceivably have been included in either of two M.A.'s, we decided its affiliation on the basis of an industrial or density gradient. The gradient of nonagricultural employment or of density (whichever was available) was examined along a line connecting the two cities. The low point in the gradient was then taken as the dividing line between the two M.A.'s.

In countries where the industrial composition of the labor force was not obtainable for minor administrative divisions, a criterion based on population density was substituted for the one based on nonagricultural employment. The density rule specifies that an administrative division may be included in the M.A. if (1) it is contiguous to the central city and has at least half the population density of the city or has at least twice the density of the next more distant ring of administrative divisions, or (2) it is not contiguous to the central city but has at least half the density of the ring of administrative divisions next nearer to the city or at least twice the density of the next more distant ring of administrative divisions.

Application of these standards begins by grouping administrative units into rings of territory around a principal city. If such a city is surrounded by one administrative division, this division is considered to be the first ring; if it is contained in more than one division, all of these constitute the first ring. The second ring consists of those administrative divisions that touch upon the first ring, and the third ring consists of those that touch upon the second. Now, by the density rule, if an administrative division is to be included in the M.A., regardless of the ring in which it falls, it must have at least one-half the density of the ring next nearer to the city or at least twice the density of the next more distant ring. Thus, in the first ring, an included administrative district must manifest a population density either half as high as that of the principal city itself or twice that of the second ring. In the second ring, an included division must have one-half the density of the first ring or twice the density of the third; and so on.

Regardless of its population density, an administrative area cannot be included in the M.A. unless it touches on the principal city or on another area that has already been included. An M.A. thus embraces a continuous territory with none of its parts physically separated from the rest. Although it is possible for several rings about a city to be included in the M.A. on either the density or the nonagricultural basis, the distance from the principal city was always taken into account.

The density requirement just described is different in one respect from that stipulated by the United States for its S.M.A.'s. The latter sets up an absolute standard—150 or more persons per square mile. This project, in contrast, employs a relative standard. The inclusion or exclusion of an administrative unit does not depend on a fixed density figure but on the comparative densities within the region considered. Such a modification is necessary, because there is great variation between one country and another with respect to average population density and with respect to urban and rural densities. Some countries, such as India and Egypt, regularly have more than 500 persons per square mile in areas that are strictly rural and agricultural. Although the average population densities within cities (from 4,000 to 100,000 per square mile) clearly exceed anything that is possible in a purely agricultural region, the lower limit of what is an urban density varies markedly from one country to another, depending in part upon the technological base. An advanced industrial country tends to have low population density both in the periphery of its metropolitan areas and in the farming sections, whereas a nonindustrial country tends to have high densities in both areas. Our relative standard, which reasons in terms of comparative densities among the administrative units surrounding a principal city, seems to be a suitable type of density criterion for purposes of international comparison.

The Procedural Steps

In applying the criteria, we took the following steps:

1) Within the country, each corporate city or continuous urban area of 50,000 or more inhabitants was located and listed as of the last census before 1954.

2) The administrative divisions surrounding these cities or urban areas were then located on a map.

3) The smallest administrative divisions around each city were designated as county equivalents, and an effort was made to determine the industrial composition of their labor force in the census reports. If the industrial composition could not be determined, data on land area and population were sought in order to obtain the population densities. If neither labor force nor density data could be found for the smallest administrative divisions around the principal city, the next largest division was taken as the county equivalent and the search for data begun anew.

4) Once the divisions with usable data were determined, the investigator worked outward from the principal city. He applied the nonagricultural or the density criterion (the first if data were available) to each successive ring of administrative units. If none of the units in the first ring about the city qualified for inclusion in the M.A., all other rings were automatically excluded, in which case the boundary of the principal city itself, or the continuous urban area, was taken to be the boundary of the M.A. If some or all units in the first ring qualified for inclusion, then the second-ring units touching on the qualifying first-ring units were examined for inclusion or exclusion.

5) After the boundaries of the M.A.'s in a particular country were thus tentatively established, a reëxamination of the boundaries was made from the standpoint of distance. All administrative divisions that appeared to be too remote from the

[30]

principal city to participate directly in its economic life, were dropped.

6) When the boundaries of each M.A. were finally delimited, the populations of all component units were added up to get a total for the M.A. If this total fell below 100,000, the area was excluded.

The "Hard Cases"

It was impossible to obtain the data for metropolitan delimitation in all countries. Some countries could not supply information for small administrative divisions, on the industrial composition of the labor force, or on the population-area ratio.[24] In such cases, with a few exceptions,[25] we had to give up the idea of delimiting M.A.'s. Instead, we took the population of their cities of 100,000 or more inhabitants and included these cities in our table. Where they appear in the table, they are in lowercase letters. When M.A.'s could not be delimited, the cities were included because they indicate the presence of M.A.'s, even though the data for their delimitation were not available.

The U.S.S.R. accounts for many cases where we have had to be content to give the population size of cities rather than M.A.'s. In only three instances—Moscow, Leningrad, and Baku—was it feasible to arrive at an approximation of an M.A., and the delimitations in these instances are based on available information, rather than on the systematic application of the density or nonagricultural criteria.

The other major country for which city figures had to be substituted for M.A.'s is China. Theodore Shabad supplied 1953 census figures for all Chinese cities, as explained in the appendix. It was not practicable to provide comparable figures for any date later than 1953, and the figures on Chinese cities for the years before 1953 (shown in the first column of the table) represent estimates.

[24] Census reports which as a minimum give the number of inhabitants, the land area, and the per cent of the labor force engaged in agriculture for the smallest type of political unit are particularly valuable in the type of research reported here. The practice of reporting these minimal data should, in our opinion, be encouraged in all countries.

[25] The exceptions were a few cities where, given no data on density and the number in agriculture, evidence could still be found indicating that an area greater than the city could justifiably be taken as the M.A.

Of a total of 202 countries and territories investigated, 105 proved to have at least one M.A. before 1954. However, 21 of these did not provide enough information for actual demarcation.[26] Fortunately, the countries utterly deficient in statistics for small areas are generally those that have no or very few large cities.[27] For this reason, for the years just before 1954, from a probable total of 1,046 M.A.'s in the world, we were able to delimit the approximate boundaries of 720 or 69 percent. Communist countries account for 266 of the 326 cases where only the population of a city is shown, with 230 of these 266 in China and the U.S.S.R.

If the project had been undertaken ten years ago, the list would have been less complete. In recent years census-taking has become the practice of an ever-increasing number of governments, and the awareness of urban concentration and metropolitan expansion has become more widespread. Even in the absence of census enumerations, population estimates for cities and administrative areas tend to be made.

THE USE AND INTERPRETATION OF THE M.A. FIGURES

Two population figures are shown for each M.A. in the table. The first figure is based on censuses or official estimates for a date preceding 1954 but as close to that year as possible; the second gives a census figure or an estimate (often our own) which is as up-to-date as possible, that is, for either 1954, 1955, or 1956. This provides both the most reliable and the most up-to-date figures, and, also, gives some idea of the growth of the M.A.'s.

The number of inhabitants for the two dates indicates growth when both figures represent census enumerations; however, in many instances, when census information was not available, the second figure is merely derived by an extrapolation of past rates of growth. The reliability of the estimates cannot be assessed until new census reports (most probably for 1960) are issued.

Our demarcations typically employed the smallest administrative divisions for which data could be found, yet this did not guarantee uniformity in size of component units. Besides, we had to take local circumstances into account. For example, the distance

---

[26] In three of the 21 cases it proved possible to delimit some but not all of the M.A.'s.

[27] Most of the exceptions are Communist countries.

of administrative divisions from the principal city introduced a realistic but unstandardized factor. In some countries, furthermore, the population figures used for the component units of M.A.'s were based on a *de facto* census whereas in other countries they were derived from a *de jure* census. Besides, the social and economic criteria for the inclusion of administrative divisions were not the same from one country to another. In most cases the proportion of the labor force in nonagricultural pursuits was used,[28] but in some countries the population-density criterion had to be employed instead. A further element of possible noncomparability lies in the use of place-of-work data in England and Wales, and the use of the S.M.A. boundaries in the United States[29] which are based on more types of information than are available for most countries.

In sum, neither completeness of coverage, absolute accuracy, or perfect comparability can be claimed for the figures in the table. We feel, however, that the advantages attained outweigh the inevitable defects of the data. Although the results are necessarily tentative, they at least afford one more tool in comparative research on urbanization, internal migration, economic location, and population redistribution.

---

[28] Although a nonagricultural requirement was used in the delimitation of M.A.'s, it should be noted that the metropolitan population of a country (*i.e.*, the population residing in M.A.'s) is not synonymous with the nonfarm or nonagricultural population of the country. It is logically possible for a country to have a large nonfarm or nonagricultural population without having any M.A.'s. This could happen in countries where the population is concentrated in small cities (*i.e.*, below 50,000) which are widely dispersed.

[29] Except in New England, where we accepted Bogue's delimitations of S.M.A. equivalents on a county basis. See note 17.

GUIDE TO THE TABLE AND APPENDIX

THE TABLE

Names and Coverage

The stub of the table contains the name of the country (underlined), of the M.A. (in capitals), and of its principal city or main urban concentration (in upper and lower case). Within each country the M.A.'s are listed in alphabetic order. Countries are listed according to continental regions.

The list contains all M.A.'s of more than 100,000 inhabitants that could be demarcated, and, in those 21 countries or territories where this was not possible, the cities with 100,000 or more population.

The unit which normally forms the largest population concentration within the M.A. is variously described in the census reports of different countries—as city, borough, county borough, municipality, municipal corporation, chief urban center, or otherwise. For the purposes of the study each one is regarded as the principal city of the M.A. under which it is shown. It usually has the largest population of any unit constituting the M.A., although there are a few exceptions. In Australia, for example, the more generally recognized center of the M.A. is presented even though, as a political entity, it may be slightly smaller in population than one or more of the other political entities making up the M.A.

Population Before 1954

The first column shows the number of inhabitants of each M.A. and its principal city for some date before 1954. The figures are normally derived from the last census preceding 1954, and the date of the census is given in parentheses opposite the name of each country. For countries and territories that have never had a census of population or for which census data were unobtainable, the figures represent official or unofficial estimates. If there is no letter following the date, the population figures have been derived from a census; the letter "s" indicates estimates obtained from an official or unofficial source; and "e" indicates population estimates made by IUR. Where it proved impossible to give any population figure, the letters "N.A." (for "not available") appear in the table.

Population in 1954–1956

The second column shows the number of inhabitants in each M.A. and principal city for one of three years—1954, 1955, or 1956.[30] The IUR estimates for 1955 were based on the last *two* censuses by calculating the rate of growth during the time between these censuses, and applying it to the years after the last census to get a figure for 1955. Necessarily, the assumption on which the estimates are made—that past rates of growth continued unchanged until 1955—may be wide of the mark in many cases, especially since the period covered by two censuses was more remote from 1955 in some instances than in others. This fact must be taken into consideration by users of the figures.[31] The estimates should be used in aggregate terms, not in terms of particular cities or in comparisons of two individual cities. The same cautions should be observed in using estimates for 1954, 1955, or 1956 derived from official or unofficial sources rather than IUR.

---

[30] The exceptions are countries or territories which had a census in 1957 but none before that time; in such cases the 1957 figures are used.

[31] It proved necessary in a small number of cases to assign the same rate of growth to the M.A. as that found for its principal city, or vice versa, when an estimate for only one of them could be made for the year 1955. Persons interested in differential rates of growth as between M.A.'s and their principal cities during the period from the last census to 1955 should accordingly ignore those cases in which the growth rate for the M.A. is identical with that for its city.

The most valid comparisons that can be made from the table are those based on the first column of population figures, for these have been drawn from census reports. However, the year of the last census varies from one country or territory to another, a defect which the second column of population figures remedies. Each of the two columns represents, in complementary fashion, both a gain and a sacrifice.

THE APPENDIX

The appendix gives, for each country in the table, the component units of each M.A. delimited in the study, and the sources of the population figures appearing in columns 1 and 2. When the population figure represents an estimate made by the IUR staff, the source is listed in the appendix as "IUR estimate."

Our listing of the units that comprise each M.A. should enable persons familiar with particular areas to analyze the demarcations critically and, we hope, suggest improvements for later revisions.

THE POPULATION OF METROPOLITAN AREAS
AND THEIR PRINCIPAL CITIES
BY COUNTRIES AND TERRITORIES

Section I: AFRICA

Metropolitan Areas and Principal Cities*	Population, Last Census Before 1954**	Estimated Population, circa 1955**	Metropolitan Areas and Principal Cities	Population, Last Census Before 1954	Estimated Population, circa 1955
ALGERIA	(1948)	(1954)	EGYPT	(1947)	(1955e)
ALGIERS	488,893	587,570	ALEXANDRIA	919,024	1,170,000
Algiers	266,165	329,706	Alexandria	919,024	1,170,000
BÔNE	102,823	114,068	CAIRO	2,156,810	2,770,000
Bône	77,675	88,920	Cairo	2,090,654	2,650,000
CONSTANTINE	118,774	148,725	EL MAHALLA		
Constantine	80,223	111,315	EL KUBRA	115,758	140,000
			El Mahalla		
ORAN	264,421	310,146	el Kubra	115,758	140,000
Oran	244,594	274,772			
			MANSURA	101,965	130,000
			Mansura	101,965	130,000
ANGOLA	(1950)	(1955s)			
			PORT SAID	177,703	200,000
LUANDA	164,340	220,000[a]	Port Said	177,703	200,000
Luanda	141,647	189,590			
			SUEZ	107,244	120,000
			Suez	107,244	120,000
BELGIAN CONGO	(1953s)	(1955e)			
			TANTA	139,926	170,000
ÉLISABETHVILLE	128,597	150,000	Tanta	139,926	170,000
Élisabethville	128,597	150,000			
LÉOPOLDVILLE	283,859	355,000			
Léopoldville	283,859	355,000			

* The name of each Metropolitan Area is capitalized and its principal city is given immediately below. In countries where it proved impossible to delimit Metropolitan Areas only the population of cities of 100,000 or more inhabitants is shown. Countries or territories having no Metropolitan Areas or cities of 100,000 or more inhabitants are not shown.

** Where no letter appears after the date in this column, the population figures shown below the date are based on a census. The letter "s" after a date in this column signifies that all of the population figures are estimates drawn from an official or unofficial source, with the source being shown in the appendix. In those cases where the letter "e" appears after the date in this column, the population figures shown below the date are estimates made by International Urban Research.

a IUR estimate.

[37]

Metropolitan Areas and Principal Cities	Population, Last Census Before 1954	Estimated Population, circa 1955
ETHIOPIA & ERITREA	(1952)	(1955e)
ADDIS ABABA	401,915	450,000
Addis Ababa	401,915	450,000
ASMARA	120,000a	130,000
Asmara	120,000a	130,000
FRENCH WEST AFRICA	(1946s)	(1955)
ABIDJAN	46,000	127,585
Abidjan	46,000	127,585
DAKAR	171,200	230,887
Dakar	130,000	185,876
GHANA	(1948)	(1955e)
ACCRA	224,771	286,000
Accra	135,926	186,000
KENYA	(1948)	(1955s)
NAIROBI	118,976	197,500
Nairobi	118,976	197,500
LIBYA	(1936)	(1954)
TRIPOLI	101,851	130,238
Tripoli	101,851	130,238
MADAGASCAR	(1951)	(1955e)
TANANARIVE	256,800	302,000
Tananarive	182,982	215,000
MOROCCO	(1951/52)	(1955e)
Casablanca	682,388	750,000a
Fez	179,372	185,000
Marrakesh	213,312	220,000
Meknes	140,380	155,000
Rabat--Salé	202,791b	220,000b
TANGIER	172,000a	183,000a
Tangier	150,000c	161,000
NIGERIA	(1952)	(1955e)
IBADAN	460,185	465,000
Ibadan	414,390	420,000
IFE	110,819	123,000
Ife	110,819	123,000
IWO	100,006	106,000
Iwo	100,006	106,000
NIGERIA (cont'd)	(1952)	(1955e)
KANO	131,316	132,000
Kano	94,159	95,000
LAGOS	358,279	393,000
Lagos	271,800	299,000
OGBOMOSHO	139,535	147,000
Ogbomosho	139,535	147,000
OSHOGBO	122,746	131,000
Oshogbo	122,746	131,000
RHODESIA & NYASALAND	(1951e)	(1956e)
BULAWAYO	120,000	140,000
Bulawayo	108,000	120,000
SALISBURY	155,000	210,000
Salisbury	120,000	140,000
SUDAN	(1953s)	(1955/56)
KHARTOUM--OMDURMAN	255,000a	260,214
Khartoum	75,000	93,103
TANGANYIKA	(1952)	(1957)
DAR-ES-SALAAM	99,140	128,740
Dar-es-Salaam	99,140	128,740
TUNISIA	(1946)	(1956)
TUNIS	414,800	470,000d
Tunis	364,593	410,000
UNION OF SOUTH AFRICA	(1951)	(1955e)
BLOEMFONTEIN	130,483	160,000
Bloemfontein	80,732	95,000
CAPE TOWN	635,369	760,000
Cape Town	441,209	495,000
DURBAN	522,451	640,000
Durban	434,548	490,000
EAST LONDON	133,102	140,000
East London	90,680	95,000
JOHANNESBURG	1,606,924	1,825,000
Johannesburg	631,911	827,500e
PORT ELIZABETH	215,819	265,000
Port Elizabeth	169,360	210,000
PRETORIA	390,526	470,000
Pretoria	231,710	250,000
VEREENIGING--VANDERBIJLPARK	153,136	225,000
Vereeniging	59,878	72,000

a Official estimate; b Total for Rabat (1951/52: 156,209; 1955: 170,000) and Salé (1951/52: 46,582; 1955: 50,000) municipalities; c IUR estimate; d IUR estimate; e Official estimate.

Metropolitan Areas and Principal Cities	Population, Last Census Before 1954	Estimated Population, circa 1955	Metropolitan Areas and Principal Cities	Population, Last Census Before 1954	Estimated Population, circa 1955
CANADA	(1951)	(1956)	UNITED STATES(cont'd)	(1950)	(1956e)
CALGARY	195,352	237,886	ATLANTIC CITY,N.J.	132,399	135,500
Calgary	129,060	181,780	Atlantic City	61,657	61,000
EDMONTON	226,199	323,539	AUGUSTA, GA.	162,013	215,000
Edmonton	159,631	226,002	Augusta	71,508	85,000
HALIFAX	162,217	197,943	AUSTIN, TEXAS	160,980	190,000
Halifax	85,589	93,301	Austin	132,459	175,000
HAMILTON	310,086	384,535	BALTIMORE, MD.	1,337,373	1,488,300
Hamilton	208,321	239,625	Baltimore	949,708	966,000
LONDON	162,139	190,897	BATON ROUGE, LA.	158,236	207,900
London	95,343	101,693	Baton Rouge	125,629	165,000
MONTREAL	1,454,645	1,713,662	BEAUMONT--		
Montreal	1,021,520	1,109,439	PORT ARTHUR,TEX.	195,083	228,000
			Beaumont	94,014	110,000
OTTAWA	334,829	392,463	BINGHAMTON, N.Y.	184,698	203,500
Ottawa	202,045	222,129	Binghamton	80,674	84,500
QUEBEC	296,515	335,593	BIRMINGHAM, ALA.	558,928	594,500
Quebec	164,016	170,703	Birmingham	326,037	345,000
TORONTO	1,319,383	1,632,149	BOSTON--LAWRENCE--		
Toronto	675,754	667,706	LOWELL, MASS.	2,875,876	2,966,000
			Boston	801,444	720,000
VANCOUVER	649,238	767,921			
Vancouver	344,833	365,844	BRIDGEPORT--		
			STAMFORD--		
VICTORIA	215,003	256,355	NORWALK, CONN.	504,342	576,800
Victoria	51,331	54,584	Bridgeport	158,709	160,000
WINDSOR	217,150	246,901	BROCKTON, MASS.	189,468	217,000
Windsor	120,049	121,980	Brockton	62,860	62,500
WINNIPEG	441,458	501,931	BUFFALO, N.Y.	1,089,230	1,231,500
Winnipeg	235,710	255,093	Buffalo	580,132	585,000
			CANTON, OHIO	283,194	317,100
UNITED STATES	(1950)	(1956e)	Canton	116,912	121,500
AKRON, OHIO	410,032	466,200	CEDAR RAPIDS,IOWA	104,274	122,800
Akron	274,605	295,000	Cedar Rapids	72,296	79,500
ALBANY--			CHARLESTON, S.C.	164,856	190,000
SCHENECTADY--			Charleston	70,174	68,000
TROY, N.Y.	514,490	561,000			
Albany	134,995	141,500	CHARLESTON, W. VA.	322,072	342,100
			Charleston	73,501	75,000
ALBUQUERQUE,N.MEX.	145,673	206,000			
Albuquerque	96,815	152,000	CHARLOTTE, N.C.	197,052	227,000
			Charlotte	134,042	150,000
ALLENTOWN--					
BETHLEHEM--			CHATTANOOGA, TENN.	246,453	268,700
EASTON, PA.	437,824	474,200	Chattanooga	131,041	137,000
Allentown	106,756	111,000			
			CHICAGO, ILL.	5,495,364	6,121,600
ALTOONA, PA.	139,514	132,000	Chicago	3,620,962	3,700,000
Altoona	77,177	73,500			
			CINCINNATI, OHIO	904,402	1,005,500
ASHEVILLE, N.C.	124,403	132,000	Cincinnati	503,998	525,000
Asheville	53,000	54,500			
			CLEVELAND, OHIO	1,465,511	1,668,600
ATLANTA, GA.[a]	671,797	828,400	Cleveland	914,808	935,000
Atlanta	331,314	495,000			

[a] See footnote at end of Section II.

[39]

Metropolitan Areas and Principal Cities	Population, Last Census Before 1954	Estimated Population, circa 1955	Metropolitan Areas and Principal Cities	Population, Last Census Before 1954	Estimated Population, circa 1955
UNITED STATES(cont'd)(1950)		(1956e)	UNITED STATES(cont'd)(1950)		(1956e)
COLUMBIA, S.C.	142,565	171,400	GREENSBORO--		
Columbia	86,914	107,000	HIGH POINT, N.C.	191,057	214,400
			Greensboro	74,389	83,000
COLUMBUS, GA.	170,541	185,900			
Columbus	79,611	86,000	GREENVILLE, S.C.	168,152	194,000
			Greenville	58,161	69,000
COLUMBUS, OHIO	503,410	610,000			
Columbus	375,901	430,000	HAMILTON--		
			MIDDLETOWN,OHIO	147,203	175,200
CORPUS CHRISTI,TEX.	165,471	211,100	Hamilton	57,951	67,200
Corpus Christi	108,287	160,000			
			HARRISBURG, PA.	292,241	343,000
DALLAS, TEXAS	614,799	755,000	Harrisburg	89,544	93,500
Dallas	434,462	570,000			
			HARTFORD--NEW		
DAVENPORT, IOWA--			BRITAIN--		
ROCK ISLAND--			BRISTOL, CONN.	539,661	616,700
MOLINE, ILL.	234,256	263,700	Hartford	177,397	179,500
Davenport	74,549	81,000			
			HOUSTON, TEXAS	806,701	1,077,000
DAYTON, OHIO	457,333	542,700	Houston	596,163	710,000
Dayton	243,872	280,000			
			HUNTINGTON, W.VA.--		
DENVER, COLO.	563,832	724,000	ASHLAND, KY.	245,795	267,400
Denver	415,786	500,000	Huntington	86,353	94,000
DES MOINES, IOWA	226,010	257,800	INDIANAPOLIS, IND.	551,777	632,600
Des Moines	177,965	190,000	Indianapolis	427,173	450,000
DETROIT, MICH.	3,016,197	3,570,000	JACKSON, MICH.	107,925	121,700
Detroit	1,849,568	1,905,000	Jackson	51,088	52,500
DULUTH, MINN.--			JACKSON, MISS.	142,164	160,700
SUPERIOR, WIS.	252,777	266,100	Jackson	98,271	118,000
Duluth	104,511	109,000			
			JACKSONVILLE, FLA.	304,029	386,400
DURHAM, N.C.	101,639	115,000	Jacksonville	204,517	245,000
Durham	71,311	79,000			
			JOHNSTOWN, PA.	291,354	292,500
EL PASO, TEXAS	194,968	247,800	Johnstown	63,232	61,000
El Paso	130,485	210,000			
			KALAMAZOO, MICH.	126,707	147,000
ERIE, PA.	219,388	236,000	Kalamazoo	57,704	66,000
Erie	130,803	134,000			
			KANSAS CITY, MO.	814,357	965,000
EVANSVILLE, IND.[a]	160,422	174,900	Kansas City	456,622	495,000
Evansville	128,636	138,000			
			KNOXVILLE, TENN.	337,105	372,000
FALL RIVER--NEW			Knoxville	124,769	135,000
BEDFORD, MASS.	381,569	390,000			
Fall River	111,963	104,000	LANCASTER, PA.	234,717	252,000
			Lancaster	63,774	66,000
FLINT, MICH.	270,963	341,000			
Flint	163,143	180,000	LANSING, MICH.	172,941	204,000
			Lansing	92,129	100,000
FORT WAYNE, IND.	183,722	212,000			
Fort Wayne	133,607	144,000	LEXINGTON, KY.	100,746	118,500
			Lexington	55,534	56,000
FORT WORTH, TEXAS	361,253	462,200			
Fort Worth	278,778	350,000	LINCOLN, NEBR.	119,742	128,900
			Lincoln	98,884	106,000
FRESNO, CALIF.	276,515	317,000			
Fresno	91,669	110,000	LITTLE ROCK--NORTH		
			LITTLE ROCK, ARK.	196,685	228,500
GALVESTON, TEXAS	113,066	134,000	Little Rock	102,213	117,000
Galveston	66,568	75,000			
			LORAIN--ELYRIA,		
GRAND RAPIDS,MICH.	288,292	338,000	OHIO	148,162	183,900
Grand Rapids	176,515	188,000	Lorain	51,202	57,000

[a] See footnote at end of Section II.

Metropolitan Areas and Principal Cities	Population, Last Census Before 1954	Estimated Population, circa 1955
UNITED STATES(cont'd)(1950)		(1956e)
LOS ANGELES, CALIF.[a]	4,367,911	5,640,000
Los Angeles	1,970,358	2,230,000
LOUISVILLE, KY.	576,900	669,800
Louisville	369,129	410,000
LUBBOCK, TEXAS	101,048	146,500
Lubbock	71,747	120,000
MACON, GA.	135,043	153,700
Macon	70,252	76,000
MADISON, WIS.	169,357	186,000
Madison	96,056	107,000
MANCHESTER, N.H.	156,987	165,400
Manchester	82,732	85,000
MEMPHIS, TENN.	482,393	553,900
Memphis	396,000	455,000
MIAMI, FLA.	495,084	710,000
Miami	249,276	260,000
MILWAUKEE, WIS.[a]	871,047	975,000
Milwaukee	637,392	710,000
MINNEAPOLIS-- ST. PAUL,MINN.	1,116,509	1,243,500
Minneapolis	521,718	540,000
MOBILE, ALA.	231,105	272,000
Mobile	129,009	170,000
MONTGOMERY, ALA.	138,965	147,000
Montgomery	106,525	117,500
NASHVILLE, TENN.	321,758	368,100
Nashville	174,307	185,000
NEW HAVEN-- WATERBURY,CONN.	545,784	601,300
New Haven	164,443	161,500
NEW ORLEANS, LA.	685,405	783,900
New Orleans	570,445	630,000
NEW YORK-- NORTHEASTERN NEW JERSEY	12,911,994	14,280,500
New York City	7,891,957	7,850,000
NORFOLK-- PORTSMOUTH,VA.	446,200	533,000
Norfolk	213,513	300,000
OKLAHOMA CITY,OKLA.	325,352	377,000
Oklahoma City	243,504	275,000
OMAHA, NEBR.	366,395	404,800
Omaha	251,117	275,000
ORLANDO, FLA.	114,950	165,000
Orlando	52,367	69,000
PEORIA, ILL.	250,512	274,000
Peoria	111,856	115,000
UNITED STATES(cont'd)(1950)		(1956e)
PHILADELPHIA,PA.	3,671,048	4,089,700
Philadelphia	2,071,605	2,140,000
PHOENIX, ARIZ.	331,770	465,000
Phoenix	106,818	160,000
PITTSBURGH, PA.	2,213,236	2,318,500
Pittsburgh	676,806	680,000
PITTSFIELD, MASS.	132,966	140,000
Pittsfield	53,348	55,700
PORTLAND, MAINE	169,201	175,000
Portland	77,634	78,500
PORTLAND, OREGON	704,829	778,000
Portland	373,628	402,000
PROVIDENCE, R.I.	681,815	701,000
Providence	248,674	225,000
RACINE, WIS.	109,585	122,000
Racine	71,193	78,000
RALEIGH, N.C.	136,450	146,500
Raleigh	65,679	72,000
READING, PA.	255,740	255,000
Reading	109,320	105,000
RICHMOND, VA.	328,050	363,900
Richmond	230,310	240,000
ROANOKE, VA.	133,407	144,500
Roanoke	91,921	99,000
ROCHESTER, N.Y.	487,632	536,000
Rochester	332,488	342,000
ROCKFORD, ILL.	152,385	179,000
Rockford	92,927	113,000
SACRAMENTO, CALIF.	277,140	385,000
Sacramento	137,572	158,000
SAGINAW, MICH.	153,515	176,500
Saginaw	92,918	102,500
ST. LOUIS, MO.	1,681,281	1,891,000
St. Louis	856,796	840,000
SALT LAKE CITY, UTAH	274,895	323,500
Salt Lake City	182,121	207,000
SAN ANTONIO, TEXAS	500,460	563,800
San Antonio	408,442	485,000
SAN BERNARDINO, CALIF.[a]	281,642	383,000
San Bernardino	63,058	83,000
SAN DIEGO, CALIF.	556,808	825,000
San Diego	334,387	480,000
SAN FRANCISCO-- OAKLAND,CALIF.	2,240,767	2,583,500
San Francisco	775,357	790,000

[a] See footnote at end of Section II.

Metropolitan Areas and Principal Cities	Population, Last Census Before 1954	Estimated Population, circa 1955	Metropolitan Areas and Principal Cities	Population, Last Census Before 1954	Estimated Population, circa 1955
UNITED STATES(cont'd)(1950)		(1956e)	UNITED STATES(cont'd)(1950)		(1956e)
SAN JOSE, CALIF.	290,547	440,000	TOLEDO, OHIO	395,551	443,700
San Jose	95,280	121,000	Toledo	303,616	327,000
SAVANNAH, GA.	151,481	168,300	TOPEKA, KANSAS	105,418	118,500
Savannah	119,638	131,000	Topeka	78,791	85,000
SCRANTON, PA.	257,396	245,000	TRENTON, N.J.	229,781	245,000
Scranton	125,536	120,000	Trenton	128,009	130,000
SEATTLE, WASH.	732,992	800,000	TULSA, OKLA.	251,686	297,700
Seattle	467,591	560,000	Tulsa	182,740	215,000
SHREVEPORT, LA.[a]	176,547	198,400	UTICA--ROME,N.Y.	284,262	305,900
Shreveport	127,206	152,000	Utica	101,531	104,000
SIOUX CITY, IOWA	103,917	104,100	WACO, TEXAS	130,194	149,400
Sioux City	83,991	85,500	Waco	84,706	106,000
SOUTH BEND, IND.	205,058	231,400	WASHINGTON,D.C.	1,464,089	1,885,300
South Bend	115,911	127,000	Washington	802,178	859,000
SPOKANE, WASH.	221,561	255,000	WATERLOO, IOWA	100,448	118,500
Spokane	161,721	185,000	Waterloo	65,198	74,000
SPRINGFIELD, ILL.	131,484	138,500	WHEELING, W.VA.-- STEUBENVILLE, OHIO	354,092	357,600
Springfield	81,628	85,000	Wheeling	58,891	58,000
SPRINGFIELD, MO.	104,823	116,400	WICHITA, KANSAS	222,290	302,000
Springfield	66,731	80,500	Wichita	168,279	235,000
SPRINGFIELD, OHIO	111,661	125,000	WILKES-BARRE-- HAZLETON, PA.	392,241	360,000
Springfield	78,508	83,500	Wilkes-Barre	76,826	70,000
SPRINGFIELD-- HOLYOKE, MASS.	455,565	495,200	WILMINGTON, DEL.	268,387	330,600
Springfield	162,399	167,000	Wilmington	110,356	110,000
STOCKTON, CALIF.	200,750	229,500	WINSTON-SALEM,N.C.	146,135	161,800
Stockton	70,953	82,000	Winston-Salem	87,811	93,000
SYRACUSE, N.Y.	341,719	386,000	WORCESTER, MASS.	546,401	587,000
Syracuse	220,583	215,000	Worcester	203,486	202,000
TACOMA, WASH.	275,876	301,500	YORK, PA.	202,737	226,000
Tacoma	143,673	157,000	York	59,953	62,000
TAMPA--ST. PETERSBURG,FLA.	409,143	548,200	YOUNGSTOWN, OHIO	528,498	588,000
Tampa	124,681	250,000	Youngstown	168,330	180,000
TERRE HAUTE, IND.	105,160	105,100			
Terre Haute	64,214	64,500			

[a] Since 1950, official changes in S.M.A. boundaries have included
(1) the addition of one county to each of the following S.M.A.'s: ATLANTA (Clayton co., Ga.; 1950 pop. 22,872; 1956 pop. 28,600); EVANSVILLE (Henderson co., Ky.; 1950 pop. 30,715; 1956 pop. 34,400); MILWAUKEE (Waukesha co., Wis.; 1950 pop. 85,901; 1956 pop. 107,000); SAN BERNARDINO, whose S.M.A. name was changed to SAN BERNARDINO--RIVERSIDE--ONTARIO (Riverside co., Calif.; 1950 pop. 170,046; 1956 pop. 220,000); and SHREVEPORT (Bossier parish, La.; 1950 pop. 40,139; 1956 pop. 44,200);
(2) change of the S.M.A. name from LOS ANGELES to LOS ANGELES--LONG BEACH; and
(3) the establishment of a number of new S.M.A.'s, two of which would have qualified for this study in 1950 but were not officially recognized as S.M.A.'s until a central city in each case reached 50,000 population through annexation of territory. These two S.M.A.'s are HAMPTON--NEWPORT NEWS--WARWICK, Va. comprised of the three Independent Cities named (1950 S.M.A. pop. 143,227; 1956 pop. 177,500; chief city Newport News: 1950 pop. 42,358; 1956 pop. 44,000); and TUCSON, Ariz., comprised of Pima co. (1950 pop. 141,216; 1956 pop. 208,000; Tucson's 1950 pop. was 45,454; 1956 pop. 85,000).

Metropolitan Areas and Principal Cities	Population, Last Census Before 1954	Estimated Population, circa 1955	Metropolitan Areas and Principal Cities	Population, Last Census Before 1954	Estimated Population, circa 1955
COSTA RICA	(1950)	(1955s)	MEXICO (cont'd)	(1950)	(1955e)
SAN JOSÉ	159,150	179,225	LEÓN	157,343	195,000
San José	86,909	97,449	León	122,726	160,000
			MÉRIDA	159,410	190,000
CUBA	(1953)	(1955e)	Mérida	142,856	170,000
CAMAGÜEY	110,388	120,000	MEXICO CITY	2,960,120	3,900,000
Camagüey	110,388	120,000	Mexico City	2,234,795	2,800,000
HAVANA	1,240,369	1,315,000	MONTERREY	367,663	500,000
Havana	787,765	815,000	Monterrey	333,422	450,000
SANTIAGO DE CUBA	166,384	180,000	PUEBLA	250,961	320,000
Santiago de Cuba	163,237	175,000	Puebla	214,787	270,000
			SAN LUIS POTOSÍ	155,238	200,000
DOMINICAN REPUBLIC	(1950)	(1955e)	San Luis Potosí	125,662	165,000
CIUDAD TRUJILLO	239,464	295,000	TAMPICO	137,685	155,000
Ciudad Trujillo	181,553	240,000	Tampico	94,345	105,000
			TORREÓN--		
EL SALVADOR	(1950)	(1955s)	GÓMEZ PALACIO	231,673	295,000
			Torreón	128,971	170,000
SAN SALVADOR	220,929	270,000[a]	VERACRUZ	110,443	135,000
San Salvador	161,951	203,796	Veracruz	101,221	125,000
GUATEMALA	(1950)	(1955e)			
			NICARAGUA	(1950)	(1956e)
GUATEMALA CITY	294,344	370,000	MANAGUA	140,334	180,000
Guatemala City	284,276	360,000	Managua	109,352	145,000
HAITI	(1950)	(1955e)			
			PANAMA	(1950)	(1955e)
PORT-AU-PRINCE	216,170	235,000	PANAMA CITY	192,906	225,000
Port-au-Prince	134,117	145,000	Panama City	127,874[b]	205,000
HONDURAS	(1950)	(1955e)			
			PUERTO RICO	(1950)	(1955e)
TEGUCIGALPA	99,948	120,000			
Tegucigalpa	72,385	95,000	PONCE	126,810	140,000
			Ponce	99,492	125,000
MEXICO	(1950)	(1955e)			
			SAN JUAN	465,741	590,000
AGUASCALIENTES	118,434	125,000	San Juan	224,767[c]	440,000
Aguascalientes	93,358	100,000			
CHIHUAHUA	112,466	140,000	WEST INDIES, BRITISH (1946)		(1955s)
Chihuahua	86,961	110,000	KINGSTON	323,000[d]	346,060
			Kingston	143,000[d]	158,702
CIUDAD JUÁREZ	131,308	180,000			
Ciudad Juárez	122,566	165,000	PORT-OF-SPAIN	175,289	240,000[e]
			Port-of-Spain	92,793	120,000
GUADALAJARA	413,629	530,000			
Guadalajara	377,016	490,000			

[a] IUR estimate; [b] 1950 population within urban limits as extended in 1953: 174,600; [c] Population within urban limits as extended in 1950: 357,205; [d] 1953 figures; [e] IUR estimate.

Metropolitan Areas and Principal Cities	Population, Last Census Before 1954	Estimated Population, circa 1955	Metropolitan Areas and Principal Cities	Population, Last Census Before 1954	Estimated Population, circa 1955
ARGENTINA	(1947)	(1955e)	**BRAZIL** (cont'd)	(1950)	(1955e)
BAHÍA BLANCA	122,059	150,000	PÔRTO ALEGRE	433,977	530,000
Bahía Blanca	112,597	140,000	Pôrto Alegre	375,049	460,000
BUENOS AIRES	4,723,918	5,750,000	RECIFE	692,498	860,000
Buenos Aires	2,982,580	3,575,000	Recife	512,370	630,000
CÓRDOBA	386,828	490,000	RIO DE JANEIRO	3,052,012	3,750,000
Córdoba	369,886	470,000	Rio de Janeiro	2,303,063	2,900,000
LA PLATA	302,073	375,000	SALVADOR	417,235	500,000
La Plata	207,031	255,000	Salvador	389,422	450,000
MAR DEL PLATA	123,811	165,000	SANTOS	248,449	285,000
Mar del Plata	114,729	155,000	Santos	198,405	235,000
MENDOZA	219,034	270,000	SÃO LUÍS	119,785	140,000
Mendoza	97,496	115,000	São Luís	79,731	95,000
PARANÁ	148,106	175,000	SÃO PAULO	2,448,938	3,300,000
Paraná	84,153	110,000	São Paulo	2,017,025	2,600,000
ROSARIO	529,801	630,000			
Rosario	467,937	575,000	**BRITISH GUIANA**	(1946)	(1956e)
SAN JUAN	121,895	155,000	GEORGETOWN	94,035	120,000
San Juan	82,410	100,000	Georgetown	73,509	80,000
SANTA FE	206,212	270,000			
Santa Fe	168,791	225,000	**CHILE**	(1952)	(1955e)
TUCUMÁN	203,555	245,000	CONCEPCIÓN--		
Tucumán	194,166	235,000	TALCAHUANO	220,391	245,000
			Concepción	120,099	135,000
BOLIVIA	(1950)	(1955e)	SANTIAGO	1,423,623	1,600,000
			Santiago[a]	666,679	680,000
LA PAZ	346,130	395,000			
La Paz	321,073	370,000	VALPARAÍSO	315,506	335,000
			Valparaíso	218,829	225,000
BRAZIL	(1950)	(1955e)			
BELÉM	254,949	295,000	**COLOMBIA**	(1951)	(1955e)
Belém	225,218	270,000	BARRANQUILLA	308,713	380,000
BELO HORIZONTE	352,724	450,000	Barranquilla	276,199	340,000
Belo Horizonte	338,585	440,000	BOGOTÁ	715,250	900,000
CAMPINAS	152,547	170,000	Bogotá	638,562	806,000
Campinas	99,156	120,000	BUCARAMANGA	112,252	140,000
CURITIBA	180,575	215,000	Bucaramanga	102,887	130,000
Curitiba	138,178	165,000	CALI	284,186	385,000
FORTALEZA	270,169	335,000	Cali	241,357	330,000
Fortaleza	205,052	250,000	CARTAGENA	128,877	150,000
JOÃO PESSOA	119,326	135,000	Cartagena	111,291	130,000
João Pessoa	89,517	105,000	MANIZALES	126,201	150,000
JUIZ DE FORA	126,989	140,000	Manizales	88,893	110,000
Juiz de Fora	84,995	95,000	MEDELLÍN	441,444	565,000
MACEIÓ	120,980	140,000	Medellín	328,294	425,000
Maceió	99,088	120,000	PEREIRA	115,342	145,000
NATAL	103,215	140,000	Pereira	76,262	100,000
Natal	94,812	130,000			

[a] Comuna of Santiago only.

Metropolitan Areas and Principal Cities	Population, Last Census Before 1954	Estimated Population, circa 1955	Metropolitan Areas and Principal Cities	Population, Last Census Before 1954	Estimated Population, circa 1955
ECUADOR	(1950)	(1955e)	URUGUAY	(1950s)	(1955s)
GUAYAQUIL	266,637	320,000	MONTEVIDEO	768,413	860,306
Guayaquil	258,966	310,000	Montevideo	768,413	860,306
QUITO	212,135	255,000			
Quito	209,932	250,000	VENEZUELA	(1950)	(1955e)
			BARQUISIMETO	116,547	155,000
PARAGUAY	(1950)	(1955e)	Barquisimeto	105,108	145,000
ASUNCIÓN	206,634	235,000	CARACAS	790,456	1,000,000
Asunción	201,340	230,000	Caracas	495,064	600,000
			MARACAIBO	260,464	355,000
PERU	(1940)	(1955s)	Maracaibo	235,750	330,000
AREQUIPA	128,809	160,300	VALENCIA	101,790	120,000
Arequipa	60,725	144,000	Valencia	88,701	105,000
LIMA	645,172	1,169,000			
Lima	520,528	1,005,000			

Section V: ASIA

Metropolitan Areas and Principal Cities	Population, Last Census Before 1954	Estimated Population, circa 1955	Metropolitan Areas and Principal Cities	Population, Last Census Before 1954	Estimated Population, circa 1955
ADEN COLONY	(1946)	(1955)	CEYLON	(1953)	(1955e)
ADEN	80,516	138,441	COLOMBO	778,291	829,000
Aden	36,231	54,995	Colombo	426,127	448,000
AFGHANISTAN	(1953e)	(1955e)	CHINA: MAINLAND(1922-1949s)[a]		(1953)
Kabul	300,000	310,000	Amoy(Hsiamen)	215,000	224,300
			Anking(Anching)	121,000	105,300
BURMA	(1953)	(1955e)	Anshan	220,000	548,900
Mandalay	185,867	190,000	Antung	315,000	360,000
Moulmein	102,777	108,000	Anyang	60,000	124,900
Rangoon	737,079	775,000	Canton(Kwangchow)	1,413,000	1,598,900
CAMBODIA	(1950s)	(1955e)	Changchow	125,000	296,500
Pnom Penh	363,800	392,000	Changchun	605,000	855,200
			Changsha	422,000	650,600

[a] Estimates from various sources; see Appendix.

[45]

Metropolitan Areas and Principal Cities	Population, Last Census Before 1954	Estimated Population, circa 1955	Metropolitan Areas and Principal Cities	Population, Last Census Before 1954	Estimated Population, circa 1955
CHINA: MAINLAND(1922-1949s) (cont'd)		(1953)	CHINA: MAINLAND(1922-1949s) (cont'd)		(1953)
Changshu	64,000	101,400	Kunming	255,000	698,900
Chaochow	179,000	101,300	Kweilin	142,000	145,100
Chengchow	80,000	594,700	Kweiyang	269,000	270,900
Chengtu	620,000	856,700	Lanchow	156,000	397,400
Chinchow	155,000	352,200	Liaoyang	102,000	150,000[b]
Chinkiang (Chenchiang)	217,000	201,400	Liaoyüan (Shwangliao)	N.A.	120,100
Chinwangtao	100,000	186,800	Liuchow	208,000	158,800
Chüanchow (Tsinkiang)	50,000	107,700	Loyang	77,000	171,200
Chuchow	N.A.	127,300	Luchow(Luhsien)	74,000	289,000
Chungking (Chungching)	1,003,000	1,772,500	Mukden(Shenyang)	1,121,000	2,299,900
Dairen(Talien)[a]	723,000	640,400	Mutankiang (Mutanchiang)	200,000	151,400
Fatshan(Fushan)	163,000	122,500	Nanchang	203,000	398,200
Foochow(Fuchow)	318,000	553,000	Nanchung	53,000	164,700
Fushun	280,000	678,600	Nanking(Nanching)	1,137,000	1,091,600
Fusin(Fuhsin)	166,000	188,600	Nanning	203,000	194,600
Hangchow	606,000	696,600	Nantung	133,000	260,400
Harbin	760,000	1,163,000	Neikiang(Neichiang)	32,000	190,200
Hengyang	181,000	235,000	Ningpo	250,000	237,500
Hofei	70,000	183,600	Paoki(Paochi)	56,000	130,100
Hoihow(Haikou)	60,000	135,300	Paoting	130,000	197,000
Huhehot(Kweisui)	103,000	148,400	Paotow	53,000	149,400
Hwainan	N.A.	286,900	Pehpei	18,000	100,000[b]
Hwangshih (Huangshihchiang)	N.A.	110,500	Peking(Peiching)	1,672,000	2,768,149
Ining(Kuldja)	N.A.	108,200	Pengpu(Pangfou)	105,000	253,000
Ipin	76,000	177,500	Penki(Penchi)	98,000	449,000
Kaifeng	303,000	299,100	Port Arthur(Lushun)[a]	141,000	126,000
Kalgan (Changchiakou)	151,000	229,300	Shanghai	4,447,000	6,204,417
Kiamusze (Chiamussu)	168,000	146,000	Shangkiu (Shangchiu)	70,000	134,400
Kirin(Chilin)	239,000	435,400	Shaohing(Shaohsing)	178,000	130,600
Kokiu(Kochiu)	50,000	159,700	Shaoyang	76,000	117,700
			Shihkiachwang (Shihchiachuang)	217,000	373,400

[a] Lüshun (Port Arthur) and Talien (Dairen) now are comprised in a single municipality, Lüta, which also includes extensive rural areas. There is reason to doubt that the two cities are sufficiently linked with each other to constitute one metropolitan unit;
[b] IUR estimate.

Metropolitan Areas and Principal Cities	Population, Last Census Before 1954	Estimated Population, circa 1955	Metropolitan Areas and Principal Cities	Population, Last Census Before 1954	Estimated Population, circa 1955
CHINA: MAINLAND(1922-1949s) (cont'd)		(1953)	CHINA: MAINLAND(1922-1949s) (cont'd)		(1953)
Sian(Hsian)	503,000	787,300	Yangchüan	N.A.	100,000[b]
Siangtan(Hsiangtan)	83,000	183,600	Yentai(Chefoo)	140,000	116,000
Sinhailien (Hsinghailien)	77,000	207,600	Yingkow	155,000	131,400
Sinsiang (Hsinghsiang)	N.A.	170,500	CHINA: TAIWAN	(1953s)	(1955s)
Soochow(Suchow)	390,000	474,000	Kaohiung	305,852	352,201
Suanhwa(Hsüanhua)	N.A.	114,100	Keelung	170,413	187,468
Suchow(Hsüchow, Tungshan)	160,000	373,200	Kiayi	132,783	139,346
			Taichung	217,008	239,490
Swatow(Shantou)	147,000	280,400	Tainan	245,559	275,004
Szeping(Ssuping)	77,000	125,900	Taipei	606,765	704,124
Taichow	66,000	159,800	HONG KONG	(1931)	(1956s)
Taiyuan	252,000	720,700	HONG KONG Victoria	849,751[c] 399,565[c]	2,535,000[d] 1,000,000[d]
Tangshan	149,000	693,300			
Tatung	80,000	228,500	INDIA	(1951)	(1955e)
Tientsin (Tienching)	1,708,000	2,693,831	AGRA Agra	375,665 333,530	425,000 375,000
Tsamkong (Chanchiang)	268,000	166,000	AHMEDABAD Ahmedabad	922,060 788,333	1,075,000 895,000
Tsinan(Chinan)	591,000	680,100	AJMER Ajmer	196,633 196,633	223,000 223,000
Tsingtao(Chingtao)	759,000	916,800	ALIGARH Aligarh	141,618 141,618	156,000 156,000
Tsitsihar (Chichihaerh)	175,000	344,700	ALLAHABAD Allahabad	332,295 302,706	370,000 330,000
Tunghwa(Tunghua)	82,000	129,100	ALLEPPEY Alleppey	116,278 116,278	140,000 140,000
Tzekung(Tzuchung)	292,000	291,300	AMRAVATI Amravati	124,064 87,099	143,000 101,000
Tzepo(Tzupo)	N.A.	184,200	AMRITSAR Amritsar	325,747 323,263	340,000 337,000
Urumchi(Tihua)	80,000	140,700	BANARAS(VARANASI) Banaras	355,777 338,481	405,000 382,000
Weifang	83,000	148,900			
Wenchow	153,000	201,600	BANGALORE Bangalore	939,465 778,977	1,275,000 1,065,000
Wuchow	207,000	110,800	BAREILLY Bareilly	208,083 190,488	215,000 195,000
Wuhan	750,000[a]	1,427,300			
Wuhu	204,000	242,100	BARODA Baroda	211,407 211,407	245,000 245,000
Wusih(Wuhsi)	272,000	581,500			
Wutungkiao (Wutungchiao)	N.A.	199,100			
Yangchow (Chiangtu)	127,000	180,200			

[a] Figure is for Hankow, one of the three cities since consolidated to form Wuhan. The other two cities were Hanyang (estimated pop. 137,000) and Wuchang (estimated pop. 174,000); [b] IUR estimate. [c] Urban area of city; [d] Boundaries not specified.

Metropolitan Areas and Principal Cities	Population, Last Census Before 1954	Estimated Population, circa 1955	Metropolitan Areas and Principal Cities	Population, Last Census Before 1954	Estimated Population, circa 1955
INDIA(cont'd)	(1951)	(1955e)	INDIA(cont'd)	(1951)	(1955e)
BHAGALPUR	114,530	125,000	JULLUNDUR	168,816	205,000
Bhagalpur	114,530	125,000	Jullundur	168,816	205,000
BHAVNAGAR	137,951	157,000	KANPUR	705,383	830,000
Bhavnagar	137,951	157,000	Kanpur	636,443	740,000
BHOPAL	102,333	117,000	KHARAGPUR	129,636	155,000
Bhopal	102,333	117,000	Kharagpur	129,636	155,000
BIKANER	130,293	132,000	KOLAR GOLD FIELDS	159,084	170,000
Bikaner	117,113	118,000	Kolar Gold Fields	159,084	170,000
BOMBAY	3,386,606	4,400,000	KOLHAPUR	136,835	163,000
Bombay	2,839,270	3,600,000	Kolhapur	136,835	163,000
CALCUTTA	5,170,830	5,700,000	KOZHIKODE	158,724	175,000
Calcutta	2,548,677	2,750,000	Kozhikode	158,724	175,000
COIMBATORE	197,755	240,000	LUCKNOW	496,861	555,000
Coimbatore	197,755	240,000	Lucknow	444,711	490,000
CUTTACK	102,505	118,000	LUDHIANA	153,795	177,000
Cuttack	102,505	118,000	Ludhiana	153,795	177,000
DEHRA DUN	144,216	193,000	MADRAS	1,726,440	2,225,000
Dehra Dun	116,404	165,000	Madras	1,416,056	1,880,000
DELHI	1,774,072	2,435,000	MADURAI	361,781	435,000
Delhi	914,790	1,190,000	Madurai	361,781	435,000
GAYA	133,700	148,000	MANGALORE	117,083	138,000
Gaya	133,700	148,000	Mangalore	117,083	138,000
GORAKHPUR	132,436	150,000	MATHURA	105,773	119,000
Gorakhpur	123,844	141,000	Mathura	98,552	110,000
GUNTUR	125,255	150,000	MEERUT	233,183	270,000
Guntur	125,255	150,000	Meerut	158,407	180,000
GWALIOR	241,577	273,000	MORADABAD	161,854	170,000
Lashkar	142,443	157,000	Moradabad	154,018	160,000
HUBLI	129,609	148,000	MYSORE	244,323	305,000
Hubli	129,609	148,000	Mysore	244,323	305,000
HYDERABAD	1,085,722	1,290,000	NAGPUR	449,099	535,000
Hyderabad	803,048	1,020,000[a]	Nagpur	449,099	535,000
INDORE	310,859	375,000	PATNA	283,479	335,000
Indore	310,859	375,000	Patna	250,285	295,000
JABALPUR	256,998	302,000	POONA	594,083	760,000
Jabalpur	203,659	240,000	Poona	480,982	625,000
JAIPUR	291,130	365,000	RAJAHMUNDRY	105,276	123,000
Jaipur	291,130	365,000	Rajahmundry	105,276	123,000
JAMNAGAR	104,419	124,000	RAJKOT	132,069	185,000
Jamnagar	104,419	124,000	Rajkot	132,069	185,000
JAMSHEDPUR	218,162	245,000	RAMPUR	134,277	160,000
Jamshedpur	193,775	217,000	Rampur	134,277	160,000
JHANSI	127,365	140,000	RANCHI	106,849	137,000
Jhansi	106,333	115,000	Ranchi	94,495	123,000
JODHPUR	180,717	210,000	SAHARANPUR	148,435	170,000
Jodhpur	180,717	210,000	Saharanpur	142,665	163,000

[a] Includes Hyderabad Cantonment (1951 pop. 57,317), annexed in 1951 after census.

Metropolitan Areas and Principal Cities	Population, Last Census Before 1954	Estimated Population, circa 1955	Metropolitan Areas and Principal Cities	Population, Last Census Before 1954	Estimated Population, circa 1955
INDIA(cont'd)	(1951)	(1955e)	INDONESIA (cont'd)	(1930)	(1956s)
SALEM	202,335	248,000	Semarang	217,796	373,900
Salem	202,335	248,000			
			Surabaja	341,675	935,700
SHAHJAHANPUR	104,835	110,000			
Shahjahanpur	98,949	104,000	Surakarta	165,484	369,800
SHOLAPUR	277,087	310,000	Tjirebon	54,079	106,700
Sholapur	266,050	298,000			
SURAT	223,182	250,000	IRAN		(1956)
Surat	223,182	250,000			
			Abadan	N.A.[d]	226,103
TANJORE	100,680	120,000			
Tanjore	100,680	120,000	Ahvaz	N.A.[d]	119,828
TIRUCHIRAPALLI	218,921	250,000	Hamadan	N.A.[d]	100,029
Tiruchirapalli	218,921	250,000			
			Isfahan	N.A.[d]	254,876
TIRUNELVELI--					
PALAYAMCOTTAI	113,486	125,000	Kermanshah	N.A.[d]	125,181
Tirunelveli	73,476	80,000			
			Mashad	N.A.[d]	242,165
TRIVANDRUM	186,931	220,000			
Trivandrum	186,931	220,000	Rasht	N.A.[d]	109,493
UJJAIN	129,817	160,000	Shiraz	N.A.[d]	169,088
Ujjain	129,817	160,000			
			Tabriz	N.A.[d]	290,195
VELLORE	106,024	126,000			
Vellore	106,024	126,000	Teheran	N.A.[d]	1,513,164
VIJAYAVADA	161,198	217,000			
Vijayavada	161,198	217,000	IRAQ	(1947)	(1955e)
VISAKHAPATNAM	108,042	131,000	BAGHDAD	523,870	580,000
Visakhapatnam	108,042	131,000	Baghdad	352,137	390,000
WARANGAL	133,130	156,000	BASRA	181,331	205,000
Warangal	129,606	152,000	Basra	101,535	115,000
			MOSUL	133,625	155,000
INDONESIA	(1930)	(1956s)	Mosul	133,625	155,000
Bandjarmasin	65,698	176,800			
			ISRAEL	(1951s)	(1955s)
Bandung	166,815	839,200			
			HAIFA	209,775	230,307
Bogor	65,431	123,800	Haifa	147,000	158,000
Djakarta	533,015[a]	1,871,200[b]	JERUSALEM		
			(Israel part)	151,953	156,266
Jogjakarta	136,649	268,300	Jerusalem	137,500	144,000
Kediri	48,567	137,500	TEL AVIV-JAFFA	519,028	571,632
			Tel Aviv-Jaffa	345,500	358,500
Makassar	84,855	360,000[c]			
Malang	86,646	281,700	JAPAN	(1950)[e]	(1955)
Medan	76,584	310,600[c]	AKITA	173,029	190,202
			Akita	173,029	190,202
Padang	52,054	116,300[c]	AOMORI	160,275	183,747
Palembang	108,145	282,900[c]	Aomori	160,275	183,747
Pontianak	45,196	121,000[c]	ASAHIGAWA	136,697	164,971
			Asahigawa	136,697	164,971

[a] Includes Meester Cornelis, annexed in 1938; [b] Reported as "Greater Djakarta"; Djakarta proper given as 1,492,100; [c] 1955; [d] No prior census; [e] 1950 populations adjusted to 1955 boundaries.

Metropolitan Areas and Principal Cities	Population, Last Census Before 1954	Estimated Population, circa 1955	Metropolitan Areas and Principal Cities	Population, Last Census Before 1954	Estimated Population, circa 1955
JAPAN(cont'd)	(1950)[a]	(1955)	JAPAN(cont'd)	(1950)[a]	(1955)
ASHIKAGA	101,672	102,078	MURORAN	130,564	148,320
Ashikaga	101,672	102,078	Muroran	110,443	123,533
FUKUI	114,876	125,304	NAGANO	143,494	152,547
Fukui	114,876	125,304	Nagano	143,494	152,547
FUKUOKA	549,599	659,422	NAGAOKA	122,034	130,785
Fukuoka	442,215	544,312	Nagaoka	122,034	130,785
GIFU--ICHINOMIYA	460,960	524,876	NAGASAKI	285,489	334,442
Gifu	224,683	259,047	Nagasaki	256,245	303,724
HACHINOE	125,458	141,771	NAGOYA	1,231,235	1,501,651
Hachinoe	125,458	141,771	Nagoya	1,083,412	1,336,780
HAKODATE	228,994	242,582	NARA	111,992	115,674
Hakodate	228,994	242,582	Nara	111,992	115,674
HAMAMATSU	234,464	276,702	NIIGATA	243,266	261,758
Hamamatsu	227,140	268,792	Niigata	243,266	261,758
HIMEJI	243,680	266,490	NIIHAMA	163,199	169,917
Himeji	229,665	252,315	Niihama	101,870	107,234
HIROSAKI	131,752	138,953	NOBEOKA	103,986	116,762
Hirosaki	131,752	138,953	Nobeoka	103,986	116,762
HIROSHIMA--KURE	555,444	640,359	NUMAZU--MISHIMA	205,527	223,194
Hiroshima	287,441	357,287	Numazu	117,423	129,287
KAGOSHIMA	229,462	274,340	ODAWARA	104,561	113,099
Kagoshima	229,462	274,340	Odawara	104,561	113,099
KANAZAWA	261,456	277,283	OITA--BEPPU	191,465	214,759
Kanazawa	261,456	277,283	Oita	98,432	112,429
KIRYU	166,744	167,932	OKAYAMA	205,025	235,754
Kiryu	115,235	116,935	Okayama	205,025	235,754
KOCHI	161,640	180,146	OKAZAKI	145,977	155,902
Kochi	161,640	180,146	Okazaki	145,977	155,902
KOFU	139,030	154,494	OMUDA	259,180	269,241
Kofu	139,030	154,494	Omuda	191,978	201,737
KUMAMOTO	290,990	332,493	ONOMICHI--MIHARA	150,627	155,532
Kumamoto	290,990	332,493	Onomichi	83,533	84,882
KURASHIKI	154,169	161,605	OSAKA--KOBE	5,348,039	6,404,749
Kurashiki	120,347	123,714	Osaka	2,015,350	2,547,316
KURUME	121,487	138,804	OTARU	178,330	188,448
Kurume	121,487	138,804	Otaru	178,330	188,448
KYOTO	1,268,260	1,373,681	SAGA	118,964	126,432
Kyoto	1,105,734	1,204,084	Saga	118,964	126,432
MAEBASHI--TAKASAKI	283,996	296,460	SAPPORO	346,761	426,620
Maebashi	163,996	171,265	Sapporo	346,761	426,620
MATSUYAMA	187,877	213,457	SASEBO	278,789	317,898
Matsuyama	187,877	213,457	Sasebo	222,246	258,221
MIYAZAKI	125,611	140,782	SENDAI	341,685	375,844
Miyazaki	125,611	140,782	Sendai	341,685	375,844
MORIOKA	127,878	142,875	SHIZUOKA--SHIMIZU	378,010	432,856
Morioka	127,878	142,875	Shizuoka	256,267	295,172

[a] 1950 populations adjusted to 1955 boundaries.

Metropolitan Areas and Principal Cities	Population, Last Census Before 1954	Estimated Population, circa 1955
JAPAN(cont'd)	(1950)[a]	(1955)
TAKAMATSU	130,489	150,550
Takamatsu	124,557	144,812
TAKAOKA	126,311	131,531
Takaoka	126,311	131,531
TOKUSHIMA	155,271	171,419
Tokushima	155,271	171,419
TOKUYAMA--KUDAMATSU	166,775	175,170
Tokuyama	65,386	70,987
TOKYO--YOKOHAMA	9,048,702	11,349,339
Tokyo	5,385,071	6,969,104
TOYAMA	185,359	201,026
Toyama	154,484	170,495
TOYOHASHI	242,498	264,444
Toyohashi	185,984	202,985
UBE--ONODA	199,768	214,647
Ube	146,891	160,020
UTSUNOMIYA	211,266	227,153
Utsunomiya	211,266	227,153
WAKAYAMA	251,217	273,249
Wakayama	197,873	220,021
YAHATA--SHIMONOSEKI--KOKURA	1,493,304	1,658,956
Yahata	235,431	268,241
YAMAGATA	155,786	160,245
Yamagata	155,786	160,245
YOKKAICHI	168,622	180,536
Yokkaichi	158,629	170,602
YOSHIWARA--FUJINOMIYA	161,220	172,215
Yoshiwara	68,456	73,473
JORDAN	(1952)	(1955e)
AMMAN	108,304	120,000
Amman	108,304	120,000
JERUSALEM (Jordan part)	46,713	50,000
Jerusalem	46,713	50,000
KASHMIR (JAMMU &)	(1941)	(1955e)
SRINAGAR	207,787	265,000
Srinagar	207,787	265,000
KOREA, NORTH	(1944)	(1955e)
Chŏngjin	184,301	250,000
Hungnam--Hamhŭng[b]	255,784	260,000
KOREA, NORTH(cont'd)	(1944)	(1956e)
Kaesŏng	88,708	150,000
Pyŏngyang	342,551	450,000
Sinŭiju	118,414	175,000
Wŏnsan	112,952	150,000
KOREA, SOUTH	(1949)	(1955)
Chŏnju	100,624	124,352
Inchŏn	265,767	321,072
Kwangju	138,883	233,358
Mokpo	111,128	113,636
Pusan	473,619	1,049,363
Seoul	1,446,019	1,574,868
Taegu	313,705	488,960
Taejŏn	126,704	173,143
KUWAIT	(1955e)	(1957)
KUWAIT	113,000	119,472
Kuwait	94,000	99,438
LEBANON	(1950s)	(1954s)
Beirut	205,842	296,029
MACAU	(1950)	(1955s)
MACAU	187,772	200,000
Macau	166,544	177,000[c]
MALAYA	(1947)	(1955e)
IPOH	155,065	208,000
Ipoh	80,894	117,000
KUALA LUMPUR	237,142	370,000
Kuala Lumpur	175,961	287,000
PENANG(GEORGE TOWN)	229,967	290,000
George Town	189,068	226,000
NEPAL	(1952-1954)	(1955e)
KATHMANDU--LALITPUR	149,268	152,000
Kathmandu	106,455	108,000

[a] 1950 populations adjusted to 1955 boundaries; [b] Adjoining cities. 1944 population of Hungnam, 143,600; of Hamhŭng, 112,184; [c] IUR estimate.

Metropolitan Areas and Principal Cities	Population, Last Census Before 1954	Estimated Population, circa 1955	Metropolitan Areas and Principal Cities	Population, Last Census Before 1954	Estimated Population, circa 1955
PAKISTAN	(1951)	(1955e)	SINGAPORE	(1947)	(1955s)
CHITTAGONG[a]	294,046	320,000	SINGAPORE	938,144	1,210,534
Chittagong	145,777	169,000	Singapore	679,659	861,500
DACCA[a]	411,279	436,000			
Dacca	276,033	293,000	SYRIA	(1953s)	(1955s)
GUJRANWALA	114,201	127,000	Aleppo(Halab)	389,942	407,613
Gujranwala	114,201	127,000			
HYDERABAD	241,801	257,000	Damascus(Esh Sham)	383,239	408,774
Hyderabad	229,412	244,000	Hama	96,264	167,507
KARACHI	1,126,417	1,318,000	Homs	127,273	132,637
Karachi	905,791	1,075,000			
LAHORE	849,476	864,000	THAILAND	(1947)	(1955e)
Lahore	789,400	803,000	BANGKOK	1,178,881	1,484,000
LYALLPUR	179,144	199,000	Bangkok	604,538	761,000
Lyallpur	179,144	199,000			
MULTAN	190,122	205,000	TURKEY	(1950)	(1955)
Multan	175,429	189,000	ADANA	117,642	172,465
PESHAWAR	151,776	157,000	Adana	117,642	172,465
Peshawar	109,715	113,000			
RAWALPINDI	153,070	167,000	ANKARA	335,039	408,029
Rawalpindi	153,070	167,000	Ankara	288,536	353,170
SIALKOT	156,415	168,000	BURSA	103,812	131,336
Sialkot	124,273	133,000	Bursa	103,812	131,336
			ESKİŞEHİR	89,869	122,755
PHILIPPINES	(1948)	(1955e)	Eskişehir	89,869	122,755
CEBU	218,445	240,000	İSTANBUL	1,024,427	1,365,363
Cebu	167,503	186,000	İstanbul	983,041	1,214,616
ILOILO	110,122	129,000	İZMİR	277,180	336,061
Iloilo	110,122	129,000	İzmir	202,997	246,619
MANILA	1,657,008	2,348,000			
Manila	983,906	1,426,000	VIETNAM, NORTH	(1951s)	(1955e)
			Haiphong	146,082	186,000
RYUKYU ISLANDS	(1950)	(1955)	Hanoi	216,900	265,000
NAHA	108,662	171,682			
Naha	77,727[b]	110,740	VIETNAM, SOUTH	(1951s)	(1955e)
			Hué	110,000[c]	123,000
SAUDI ARABIA	(1952s)	(1954s)	Saigon - Cholon[d]	1,600,000	2,000,000
Hofuf	60,000	100,000			
Jidda	80,000	100,000			
Mecca	120,000	150,000			

[a] In East Pakistan. Remaining M.A.'s are in West Pakistan; [b] Includes Shuri and Oroku, annexed since 1950. 1950 population of Naha: 44,790; [c] 1952; [d] Now under one municipal administration.

Metropolitan Areas and Principal Cities	Population, Last Census Before 1954	Estimated Population, circa 1955	Metropolitan Areas and Principal Cities	Population, Last Census Before 1954	Estimated Population, circa 1955
AUSTRIA	(1951)	(1955s)	DENMARK (cont'd)	(1950)	(1955)
GRAZ	226,453	230,086	AARHUS	156,878	168,700
Graz	226,453	230,086	Aarhus	116,167	118,943
INNSBRUCK	173,186	177,000[a]	COPENHAGEN	1,219,651	1,292,915
Innsbruck	95,055	96,297	Copenhagen	768,105	753,361
LINZ	251,038	255,000[a]	ODENSE	117,138	124,219
Linz	184,685	186,372	Odense	100,940	105,915
SALZBURG	102,927	103,301			
Salzburg	102,927	103,301	FINLAND	(1950)	(1955s)
VIENNA	1,862,212	1,865,000[a]	HELSINKI	440,842	513,606
Vienna	1,616,125[b]	1,617,615	Helsinki	369,380	414,392
			TAMPERE	129,329	144,045
BELGIUM	(1947)	(1956s)	Tampere	101,143	111,405
ANTWERP	784,313	833,177	TURKU	112,888	126,902
Antwerp	263,233	256,075	Turku	101,824	111,068
BRUSSELS	1,299,925	1,371,816			
Brussels	184,838	172,009	FRANCE	(1946)	(1954)
CHARLEROI	435,091	461,024	ANGERS	117,182	127,204
Charleroi[c]	25,894	26,006	Angers	94,408	102,142
GHENT	440,864	451,856	BORDEAUX	442,219	460,079
Ghent	166,096	162,366	Bordeaux	253,751	257,946
LIÈGE	564,364	598,056	BREST	108,305	144,480
Liège	156,208	155,670	Brest	74,991	110,713
			CLERMONT-FERRAND	170,763	179,944
BULGARIA	(1946)	(1956)	Clermont-Ferrand	108,090	113,391
Plovdiv	126,563	162,518	DIJON	121,456	139,977
			Dijon	100,664	112,844
SOFIA	530,168	725,756	DOUAI	129,171	146,786
Sofia	464,757[d]	643,737	Douai[c]	37,258	43,380
Varna(Stalin)	76,954	119,769	GRENOBLE	145,207	170,073
			Grenoble	102,161	116,440
CZECHOSLOVAKIA	(1950)	(1955s)	LE HÂVRE	159,588	200,960
Bratislava	192,896	239,488	Le Hâvre	111,004	139,810
Brno	284,946	303,678	LE MANS	124,341	138,050
Ostrava	183,662	200,946	Le Mans	100,455	111,891
Plzeň	124,339	133,298	LENS--HÉNIN-LIÉTARD	323,770	363,617
			Lens	34,342	40,753
Prague(Praha)	932,659	970,572	LILLE--ROUBAIX--TOURCOING	833,110	898,524
DENMARK	(1950)	(1955)	Lille	188,871	194,616
AALBORG	105,171	111,726	LIMOGES	113,930	112,525
Aalborg	79,806	83,210	Limoges	107,857	105,990

[a] IUR estimate; [b] Adjusted to correspond to new boundaries established in 1954. Within the political boundaries at the time of the 1951 census, the city of Vienna had 1,766,102 inhabitants; [c] See Introduction regarding central cities which have a population of less than 50,000 but have a continuous urban area with more than 50,000 population; [d] Within limits of 1956. Population within 1946 limits, 434,888 (provisional census result).

Metropolitan Areas and Principal Cities	Population, Last Census Before 1954	Estimated Population, circa 1955	Metropolitan Areas and Principal Cities	Population, Last Census Before 1954	Estimated Population, circa 1955
FRANCE(cont'd)	(1946)	(1954)	GERMANY,EAST(cont'd)(1950s)[a]		(1955s)
LYON Lyon	772,122 460,748	817,832 471,270	DRESDEN Dresden	742,100 494,200	740,600 496,500
MARSEILLE Marseille	750,245 636,264	797,873 661,492	ERFURT Erfurt	253,200 188,700	248,800 188,100
METZ Metz	136,530 70,105	172,749 85,701	GERA Gera	172,300 98,600	172,700 98,000
MONTPELLIER Montpellier	95,447 93,102	100,424 97,501	GÖRLITZ Görlitz	141,700 100,100	135,200 96,100
MULHOUSE Mulhouse	178,671 91,560	202,062 99,079	HALLE Halle	539,800 289,100	535,900 289,700
NANCY Nancy	248,294 113,477	278,634 124,797	JENA Jena	123,300 80,300	124,300 83,100
NANTES Nantes	243,585 200,265	274,951 222,790	KARL-MARX-STADT (CHEMNITZ) Karl-Marx-Stadt	 505,000 293,400	 495,200 290,200
NICE Nice	258,023 211,165	299,621 244,360	LEIPZIG Leipzig	812,700 617,600	800,900 613,700
ORLÉANS Orléans	108,041 70,240	121,048 76,439	MAGDEBURG Magdeburg	488,600 260,300	477,900 261,400
PARIS Paris	6,068,716 2,725,374	6,736,836 2,850,189	ROSTOCK Rostock	178,100 133,100	191,300 150,000
REIMS Reims	118,302 110,749	129,641 121,145	ZWICKAU Zwickau	360,300 138,800	350,700 135,800
RENNES Rennes	141,191 113,781	154,236 124,122			
ROUEN Rouen	295,748 107,739	334,837 116,540	GERMANY,WEST	(1950)	(1955s)
SAINT-ÉTIENNE Saint-Étienne	349,345 177,966	367,878 181,730	AACHEN Aachen	351,768 129,811	396,700 151,100
STRASBOURG Strasbourg	286,177 175,515	316,783 200,921	AUGSBURG Augsburg	266,826 185,183	292,800 202,700
TOULON Toulon	215,504 125,742	247,015 141,117	BERLIN, WEST West Berlin	2,146,952 2,146,952	2,195,200 2,195,200
TOULOUSE Toulouse	287,798 264,411	300,289 268,863	BERLIN, EAST AND WEST East Berlin West Berlin	 4,199,552 1,189,100 2,146,952	 4,244,600 1,139,900 2,195,200
TOURS Tours	129,478 80,044	142,846 83,618	BIELEFELD Bielefeld	254,897 153,613	288,000 172,700
GERMANY, EAST	(1950s)[a]	(1955s)	BONN Bonn	460,131 115,394	530,800 140,800
BERLIN, EAST East Berlin	2,052,600 1,189,100	2,049,400 1,139,900	BRAUNSCHWEIG Braunschweig	444,670 223,760	447,600 244,500
BERLIN, EAST AND WEST East Berlin West Berlin	 4,199,552 1,189,100 2,146,952	 4,244,600 1,139,900 2,195,200	BREMEN Bremen	616,865 444,549	666,594 508,600
DESSAU Dessau	184,300 92,000	184,500 94,300	BREMERHAVEN Bremerhaven	114,070 114,070	131,000 131,000
			COLOGNE Cologne	1,059,609 594,941	1,243,900 715,900

[a] 1950 figures are official estimates.

Metropolitan Areas and Principal Cities	Population, last Census Before 1954	Estimated Population, circa 1955	Metropolitan Areas and Principal Cities	Population, Last Census Before 1954	Estimated Population, circa 1955
GERMANY,WEST(cont'd)	(1950)	(1955s)	GERMANY,WEST(cont'd)	(1950)	(1955s)
DARMSTADT	268,356	303,600	NUREMBERG	632,293	697,800
Darmstadt	94,788	124,400	Nuremberg	362,459	419,000
DÜSSELDORF	707,635	883,200	OLDENBURG	122,809	120,800
Düsseldorf	500,516	645,500	Oldenburg i. O.	122,809	120,800
ESSEN--DORTMUND-- DUISBURG(INNER RUHR)	4,597,223	5,353,100	OSNABRÜCK	227,072	241,700
Essen	605,411	690,900	Osnabrück	109,538	126,600
FLENSBURG	181,672	156,800	PFORZHEIM	110,085	130,800
Flensburg	102,832	94,300	Pforzheim	54,143	70,800
FRANKFURT AM MAIN	1,308,531	1,520,100	REGENSBURG	117,291	124,100
Frankfurt am Main	532,037	640,000	Regensburg	117,291	124,100
FREIBURG	109,717	129,000	SAARBRÜCKEN	355,920[b]	374,024[c]
Freiburg	109,717	129,000	Saarbrücken	111,450[b]	123,329[c]
HAMBURG	1,951,988	2,107,100	SALZGITTER	100,667	99,500
Hamburg	1,605,606	1,781,500	Salzgitter	100,667	99,500
HAMM	132,883	146,000[a]	STUTTGART	1,129,111	1,336,700
Hamm	59,866	66,900	Stuttgart	497,677	602,900
HANNOVER	786,615	868,400	WIESBADEN--MAINZ	365,333	424,600
Hannover	444,296	532,200	Wiesbaden	220,741	250,200
HILDESHEIM	199,180	200,400	WILHELMSHAVEN	101,210	98,500
Hildesheim	72,292	85,800	Wilhelmshaven	101,210	98,500
KARLSRUHE	444,826	483,900	WUPPERTAL-- SOLINGEN-- REMSCHEID	763,297	849,800
Karlsruhe	198,840	222,600	Wuppertal	363,224	405,400
KASSEL	333,460	355,300	GREECE	(1951)	(1955e)
Kassel	162,132	192,500	ATHENS	1,378,586	1,490,000
KIEL	254,449	257,300	Athens	565,084	595,000
Kiel	254,449	257,300	SALONIKA	297,164	305,000
KOBLENZ	133,671	159,600	Salonika	217,049	218,000
Koblenz	66,444	87,000	HUNGARY	(1949)[d]	(1954s)
KREFELD--M.GLADBACH-- RHEYDT	597,812	668,600	Budapest	1,590,264	1,783,000
Krefeld	171,875	198,100	Debrecen	110,963	118,100
LÜBECK	345,428	319,100	Miskolc	109,146	135,200
Lübeck	238,276	228,800	IRELAND(EIRE)	(1951)	(1956)
MANNHEIM-- LUDWIGSHAFEN-- HEIDELBERG	1,145,547	1,278,400	CORK	144,661	147,134
Mannheim	245,634	290,700	Cork	82,884[e]	80,011
MUNICH	1,109,846	1,269,000	DUBLIN	668,475	680,466
Munich	831,937	968,200	Dublin	551,555[e]	539,476
MÜNSTER	209,759	248,900			
Münster	118,496	155,700			

Metropolitan Areas and Principal Cities	Population, Last Census Before 1954	Estimated Population, circa 1955
ITALY[a]	(1951)	(1956s)
BARI	275,065	307,100
Bari	268,183	299,900
BÈRGAMO	230,148	247,800
Bèrgamo	103,256	110,000
BOLOGNA	350,619	402,200
Bologna	340,526	387,600
BRÈSCIA	162,354	172,700
Brèscia	142,059	151,200
BUSTO ARSÌZIO-- LEGNANO-- GALLARATE	263,042	285,400
Busto Arsìzio	52,607	57,000
CÀGLIARI	163,034	184,400
Càgliari	138,539	155,400
CARRARA--MASSA	118,819	124,400
Carrara	62,287	64,200
CATÀNIA	303,119	341,000
Catània	299,629	337,300
COMO	106,891	112,200
Como	70,447	73,300
FLORENCE	459,342	493,300
Florence	374,625	403,900
GENOA	727,245	766,100
Genoa	688,447	727,000
LA SPÈZIA	177,009	182,600
La Spèzia	111,849	116,100
LEGHORN	142,333	152,700
Leghorn	142,333	152,700
MESSINA[a]	220,766	238,200
Messina	220,766	238,200
MILAN	1,972,980	2,153,700
Milan	1,274,245	1,355,400
MÒDENA	111,364	121,800
Mòdena[a]	111,364	121,800
NAPLES	1,429,268	1,565,100
Naples	1,010,550	1,096,800

Metropolitan Areas and Principal Cities	Population, Last Census Before 1954	Estimated Population, circa 1955
ITALY (cont'd)	(1951)	(1956s)
PADUA	177,793	194,400
Padua	167,672	183,700
PALERMO	490,692	557,500
Palermo	490,692	557,500
PARMA	122,978	126,600
Parma[a]	122,978	126,600
RÈGGIO DI CALÀBRIA	140,734	147,500
Règgio di Calàbria	140,734	147,500
ROME[b]	1,757,031	1,958,600
Rome	1,651,754	1,829,400
SALERNO	156,150	167,000
Salerno[a]	90,753	99,300
TÀRANTO	168,941	185,100
Tàranto	168,941	185,100
TRIESTE	290,538	303,300
Trieste	272,522	285,500
TURIN	870,645	1,028,300
Turin	719,300	855,200
VENICE	348,699	367,400
Venice	316,891	333,200
VERONA	189,077	206,000
Verona[a]	178,594	194,300
MALTA & GOZO	(1948)	(1955s)
VALLETTA	192,799	198,500
Valletta[c]	18,666	18,800
NETHERLANDS	(1947)	(1955s)
AMSTERDAM	936,896	1,017,042
Amsterdam	803,847	863,802
ARNHEM	153,988	180,741
Arnhem	97,350	116,421
DORDRECHT	109,030	120,985
Dordrecht	68,217	75,586

[a] The data for central cities refer to communes. Administratively, communes with large populations are generally comparable to cities elsewhere. Demographically, they usually include some small outlying communities and open-country areas, in addition to the central agglomeration. For six of the central cities listed, it appears that the commune population overstates the true urban aggregate by more than ten percent. These cities are as follows, with the 1951 population of the agglomeration itself given for comparison: Messina, 168,497; Mòdena, 75,276; Parma, 85,249; Règgio di Calàbria, 81,057; Salerno, 72,626; and Verona, 134,636. These agglomeration figures are those given in the 1951 census; they tend to understate the aggregate "urban" population of the commune, which would lie somewhere between the agglomeration figures and the commune totals given in the table. Two other communes, Ferrara and Règgio nell'Emilia, each had more than 100,000 population in 1951, but each includes so much non-urban territory that neither qualifies as an M.A.; [b] Excludes population of the Vatican City (1948 census population, 890; currently estimated at approximately 1,000); [c] See Introduction regarding central cities which have a population of less than 50,000 but have a continuous urban area with more than 50,000 population.

Metropolitan Areas and Principal Cities	Population, Last Census Before 1954	Estimated Population, circa 1955
NETHERLANDS(cont'd)	(1947)	(1955s)
EINDHOVEN	182,023	211,322
Eindhoven	134,527	151,742
ENSCHEDE--HENGELO	162,192	186,693
Enschede	101,015	115,227
GRONINGEN	147,890	158,343
Groningen	132,021	141,373
HAARLEM--VELSEN	280,868	313,935
Haarlem	156,856	166,154
HEERLEN--KERKRADE	193,391	225,243
Heerlen	56,625	64,705
LEIDEN	113,165	124,310
Leiden	86,914	93,600
NIJMEGEN	123,296	138,619
Nijmegen	106,523	118,432
ROTTERDAM	836,199	935,710
Rotterdam	646,248	712,513
THE HAGUE	687,742	766,621
The Hague	532,998	596,675
TILBURG	121,182	136,812
Tilburg	114,312	128,683
UTRECHT	333,484	372,643
Utrecht	185,246	243,884
NORWAY	(1950)	(1954s)
BERGEN	177,401	189,000
Bergen	112,845	112,607
OSLO	536,319	565,000[a]
Oslo	434,047	447,800
POLAND	(1950)	(1956s)
BYDGOSZCZ	162,524	210,900
Bydgoszcz	162,524	210,900
CZĘSTOCHOWA	112,198	154,600
Częstochowa	112,198	154,600
GDAŃSK--GDYNIA	334,800	437,000
Gdańsk	194,633	259,900
KATOWICE--ZABRZE--BYTOM(UPPER SILESIA)	1,675,000[a]	1,921,000
Katowice	175,496	203,700
KRAKÓW	343,638	463,500
Kraków	343,638	463,500

Metropolitan Areas and Principal Cities	Population, Last Census Before 1954	Estimated Population, circa 1955
POLAND(cont'd)	(1950)	(1956s)
ŁÓDŹ	768,000[a]	844,000
Łódź	620,183	681,900
LUBLIN	116,629	142,400
Lublin	116,629	142,400
POZNAŃ	320,670	376,900
Poznań	320,670	376,900
SZCZECIN	178,907	237,600
Szczecin	178,907	237,600
WAŁBRZYCH	148,000[a]	172,000
Wałbrzych	93,842	110,300
WARSAW	1,300,000[a]	1,595,000
Warsaw	803,888	1,022,900
WROCŁAW	308,925	387,900
Wrocław	308,925	387,900
PORTUGAL	(1950)	(1955e)
LISBON	1,043,385	1,130,000
Lisbon	790,434	835,000
OPORTO	606,990	640,000
Oporto	284,842	295,000
ROMANIA	(1948)	(1956)
Arad	87,291	106,457
Brăila	95,514	102,491
Bucharest (Bucureşti)	1,041,807	1,236,905
Cluj	117,915	154,752
Constanţa	78,586	99,690
Craiova	84,574	96,929
Galaţi	80,411	95,646
Iaşi	94,075	112,989
Oradea	82,282	99,007
Ploeşti	95,632	114,560
Sibiu	60,602	90,478
Stalin(Braşov)	82,984	123,882
Timişoara	111,987	142,251

[a] IUR estimate.

Metropolitan Areas and Principal Cities	Population, Last Census Before 1954	Estimated Population, circa 1955	Metropolitan Areas and Principal Cities	Population, Last Census Before 1954	Estimated Population, circa 1955
SPAIN[a]	(1950)	(1955e)	SPAIN(cont'd)	(1950)	(1955e)
ALICANTE	104,222	109,000	SEVILLE	394,575	430,000
Alicante	104,222	109,000	Seville	376,627	410,000
BARCELONA	1,527,304	1,655,000	VALENCIA	605,855	640,000
Barcelona	1,280,179	1,390,000	Valencia	509,075	535,000
BILBAO	380,863	405,000	VALLADOLID	124,212	128,000
Bilbao	229,334	252,000	Valladolid	124,212	128,000
CÁDIZ	100,249	107,000	VIGO	137,873	145,000
Cádiz	100,249	107,000	Vigo[a]	137,873	145,000
CÓRDOBA	165,403	179,000	ZARAGOZA	264,256	279,000
Córdoba[a]	165,403	179,000	Zaragoza	264,256	279,000
GIJÓN	110,985	118,000			
Gijón[a]	110,985	118,000	SWEDEN	(1950)	(1955s)
GRANADA	162,725	165,000	GÖTEBORG	426,577	458,400
Granada	154,378	156,000	Göteborg	354,381	380,442
LA CORUÑA	133,844	151,000	MALMÖ	202,036	219,600
La Coruña	133,844	151,000	Malmö	192,670	209,473
LAS PALMAS DE GRAN CANARIA[b]	153,262	172,000	STOCKHOLM	946,305	1,021,068
			Stockholm	744,431	785,945
Las Palmas de Gran Canaria[a]	153,262	172,000			
			SWITZERLAND	(1950)	(1955s)
MADRID	1,663,329	1,840,000	BASEL	298,534	326,000[d]
Madrid	1,645,215[c]	1,815,000	Basel	183,543	195,000
MÁLAGA	276,222	296,000	BERN	201,144	221,000[d]
Málaga	276,222	296,000	Bern	146,499	156,600
MURCIA	218,375	230,000	GENEVA	196,037	215,000[d]
Murcia[a]	218,375	230,000	Geneva	145,473	160,400
OVIEDO	106,002	120,000	LAUSANNE	135,508	151,000[d]
Oviedo[a]	106,002	120,000	Lausanne	106,807	114,400
PALMA DE MALLORCA	136,814	149,000	ZÜRICH	533,116	588,000[d]
Palma de Mallorca	136,814	149,000	Zürich	390,020	418,600
SAN SEBASTIÁN	149,357	157,000			
San Sebastián	113,776	118,000	UNITED KINGDOM: ENGLAND & WALES	(1951)	(1956s)
SANTA CRUZ DE TENERIFE[b]	103,446	123,000	ALDERSHOT-- FARNBOROUGH	139,925	152,020
Santa Cruz de Tenerife[a]	103,446	123,000	Aldershot	37,646	38,670
SANTANDER	102,462	103,000	BARNSLEY	190,453	190,420
Santander	102,462	103,000	Barnsley	75,630	74,830

[a] The data for central cities refer to municipios. Administratively, municipios with large populations are generally comparable to cities elsewhere. Demographically, they usually include some small outlying communities and open-country areas, in addition to the central agglomeration. For seven of the central cities listed, it appears that the municipio population overstates the true urban aggregate by more than ten percent. The urban zone of each of the municipios is somewhat larger than the official census agglomeration. For comparison with the municipio figures in the table, the estimated total population of the urban zone for each of these places is as follows (with the official census agglomeration population in parentheses): Córdoba, 147,000 (141,579); Gijón, 95,000 (86,623); Las Palmas de Gran Canaria, 134,000 (131,847); Murcia, 95,000 (57,640); Oviedo, 80,000 (71,598); Santa Cruz de Tenerife, 90,000 (75,412); and Vigo, 85,000 (51,636). Two other municipios, Cartagena and Jerez de la Frontera, each had more than 100,000 population in 1950, but each includes so much non-urban territory that neither qualifies as an M.A.; [b] In the Canary Islands; [c] Includes population (26,780) of Villaverde, annexed since 1950; [d] IUR estimate.

[58]

Metropolitan Areas and Principal Cities	Population, Last Census Before 1954	Estimated Population, circa 1955	Metropolitan Areas and Principal Cities	Population, Last Census Before 1954	Estimated Population, circa 1955
UNITED KINGDOM: ENGLAND & WALES	(1951)	(1956s)	UNITED KINGDOM: ENGLAND & WALES	(1951)	(1956s)
BIRMINGHAM	2,520,880	2,575,840	LEEDS--BRADFORD	1,909,004	1,901,420
Birmingham	1,112,685	1,110,800	Leeds	505,219	508,600
BLACKBURN--			LEICESTER	427,644	440,340
ACCRINGTON	236,663	232,260	Leicester	285,181	284,000
Blackburn	111,218	107,900			
			LIVERPOOL	1,600,853	1,624,510
BLACKPOOL	230,414	232,880	Liverpool	788,659	773,700
Blackpool	147,184	146,500			
			LONDON	10,282,928	10,490,690
BOURNEMOUTH--POOLE	252,850	256,120	London AC	3,347,982	3,273,000
Bournemouth	144,845	142,600	City of London	5,324	5,180
BRIGHTON--WORTHING	362,728	371,900	LUTON	147,124	156,050
Brighton	156,486	158,700	Luton	110,381	114,500
BRISTOL	599,017	610,420	MANCHESTER	2,509,870	2,499,210
Bristol	442,994	440,500	Manchester	703,082	686,200
BURNLEY--NELSON	180,742	175,000	MANSFIELD--SUTTON	223,545	228,460
Burnley	84,987	82,350	Mansfield	51,352	51,870
CAMBRIDGE	120,145	132,930	MIDDLESBROUGH--		
Cambridge	81,500	91,780	STOCKTON--WEST		
			HARTLEPOOL	483,367	495,610
CARDIFF--RHONDDA	590,603	596,990	Middlesbrough	147,272	149,900
Cardiff	243,632	249,800			
			NEWCASTLE UPON		
CHATHAM--ROCHESTER--			TYNE	1,128,080	1,136,910
GILLINGHAM	179,878	197,170	Newcastle upon		
Chatham	44,424	49,900	Tyne	291,724	277,100
CHESTERFIELD	200,690	215,650	NEWPORT--PONTYPOOL	414,653	415,610
Chesterfield	68,558	67,240	Newport	105,547	104,900
COVENTRY	515,929	546,750	NORTHAMPTON	141,721	143,710
Coventry	258,245	272,600	Northampton	104,432	101,800
DARLINGTON--			NORWICH	214,354	217,580
AUCKLAND	147,427	152,010	Norwich	121,236	120,300
Darlington	84,886	83,360			
			NOTTINGHAM	602,761	620,920
DERBY	358,620	365,080	Nottingham	306,055	312,500
Derby	141,267	137,500			
			OXFORD	170,858	187,880
DONCASTER	174,054	180,020	Oxford	98,684	104,500
Doncaster	82,054	83,160			
			PLYMOUTH	253,262	262,980
EXETER	132,223	135,060	Plymouth	208,012	216,200
Exeter	75,513	77,000			
			PORTSMOUTH	366,828	397,000
GLOUCESTER	103,640	109,070	Portsmouth	233,545	231,100
Gloucester	67,280	67,300			
			PORT TALBOT	134,747	139,200
GRIMSBY	136,986	139,900	Port Talbot	44,115	47,130
Grimsby	94,557	95,400			
			PRESTON	272,667	273,970
HULL, KINGSTON			Preston	119,250	117,200
UPON	334,759	339,140			
Kingston upon			READING	205,812	221,710
Hull	299,105	300,200	Reading	114,196	117,900
IPSWICH	104,785	110,300	SAINT HELENS	126,181	127,050
Ipswich	104,785	110,300	Saint Helens	110,260	110,900
LANCASTER--			SHEFFIELD	744,974	742,830
MORECAMBE	104,060	102,940	Sheffield	512,850	499,000
Lancaster	51,661	49,530			

Metropolitan Areas and Principal Cities	Population, Last Census Before 1954	Estimated Population, circa 1955	Metropolitan Areas and Principal Cities	Population, Last Census Before 1954	Estimated Population, circa 1955
UNITED KINGDOM: ENGLAND & WALES	(1951)	(1956s)	UNITED KINGDOM: SCOTLAND	(1951)	(1956s)
SOUTHAMPTON Southampton	356,525 178,343	375,090 196,400	ABERDEEN Aberdeen	211,900 182,729	216,096 186,396
STOKE ON TRENT Stoke on Trent	489,128 275,115	499,250 273,000	DUNDEE Dundee	195,096 177,340	196,644 178,536
SUNDERLAND Sunderland	232,959 181,524	235,020 182,800	EDINBURGH Edinburgh	591,300 466,761	595,649 466,889
SWANSEA--NEATH Swansea	305,057 160,988	304,000 161,700	GLASGOW Glasgow	1,878,911 1,089,767	1,896,619 1,081,665
SWINDON Swindon	105,863 68,953	114,120 74,040	GREENOCK Greenock	107,017 76,292	109,936 77,748
WARRINGTON Warrington	181,327 80,694	181,480 79,620			
WIGAN--LEIGH Wigan	299,560 84,560	296,670 82,130	YUGOSLAVIA[a]	(1953)	(1955e)
			Belgrade (Beograd)	469,988	510,000
YORK York	125,766 105,371	128,200 106,200	Ljubljana	138,211	146,000
			Sarajevo	135,657	142,000
			Skoplje	121,551	129,000
UNITED KINGDOM: NORTHERN IRELAND	(1951)	(1955e)	Zagreb	350,452	368,000
BELFAST Belfast	527,775 443,671	537,000 445,000			

[a] The city of Subotica had more than 100,000 population within its limits in 1953; however, so large a share of this population lived in outlying non-urban sections that the city does not qualify as an M.A.

Section VII: OCEANIA

Metropolitan Areas and Principal Cities	Population, Last Census Before 1954	Estimated Population, circa 1955	Metropolitan Areas and Principal Cities	Population, Last Census Before 1954	Estimated Population, circa 1955
AUSTRALIA	(1947)	(1954)	HAWAII	(1950)	(1956e)
ADELAIDE Adelaide	392,112 34,990	497,446 30,102	HONOLULU Honolulu	353,020 248,034	429,000 276,500
BRISBANE Brisbane[a]	402,030 21,391	502,320 17,938	NEW ZEALAND	(1951)[d]	(1956)
MELBOURNE Melbourne	1,275,525 99,861	1,470,000[b] 93,172	AUCKLAND Auckland	348,044 128,387	404,014 136,540
NEWCASTLE Greater Newcastle	227,488 127,138	259,776 134,079	CHRISTCHURCH Christchurch	179,143 133,498	199,388 142,711
PERTH Perth	272,528 98,890	348,647 97,350	DUNEDIN Dunedin	103,208 70,440	107,359 71,277
SYDNEY Sydney	1,626,083 213,900[c]	1,869,000[b] 193,103	WELLINGTON Wellington	214,943 124,555	232,881 122,070

[a] Brisbane Community Area. Municipality of Greater Brisbane now includes entire metropolitan area; [b] IUR estimate; [c] Includes municipalities annexed to Sydney after census. 1947 population of Sydney municipality was 95,925; [d] Where boundaries have been altered between 1951 and 1956 compensatory adjustments have been made to the 1951 figures. 1951 populations of cities within 1951 boundaries as follows: Auckland, 127,406; Christchurch, 123,548; Dunedin, 69,829; Wellington, 120,072.

Metropolitan Areas and Principal Cities	Population, Last Census Before 1954	Estimated Population, circa 1955	Metropolitan Areas and Principal Cities	Population, Last Census Before 1954	Estimated Population, circa 1955
U.S.S.R.[a]	(1939)	(1956s)	U.S.S.R.(cont'd)	(1939)	(1956s)
Alma-Ata	230,528	330,000	Izhevsk	175,740	252,000
Andizhan	83,691	115,000	Kadiyevka	68,360	170,000
Anzhero-Sudzhensk	71,079	116,000	Kalinin	216,131	240,000
Arkhangelsk	281,091	238,000	Kaliningrad	372,164[d]	188,000
Armavir	83,677	102,000	Kaluga	89,484	122,000
Ashkhabad	126,580	142,000	Kamensk-Uralskiy	50,897	122,000
Astrakhan	253,655	276,000	Karaganda	165,937	350,000
BAKU[b] Baku	809,347 N.A.	939,000 598,000	Kaunas	154,109[d]	195,000
Barnaul	148,129	255,000	Kazan	401,665	565,000
Biysk	80,190	112,000	Kemerovo	132,978	240,000
Bryansk	87,473	185,000[c]	Khabarovsk	199,364	280,000
Chelyabinsk	273,127	612,000	Kharkov	833,432	877,000
Cheremkhovo	65,907	124,000	Kherson	97,186	134,000
Chernovtsy	109,698[d]	142,000	Kiev	846,293	991,000
Chimkent	74,185	130,000	Kirov	143,181	211,000
Chita	102,555	162,000	Kirovabad[e]	98,743	111,000
Dneprodzerzhinsk	147,829	163,000	Kirovograd	100,331	115,000
Dnepropetrovsk	500,662	576,000	Kiselevsk	13,000[f]	116,000
Dzerzhinsk	103,415	147,000	Kishinev	112,500[d]	190,000
Frunze	92,659	190,000	Komsomolsk-na-Amure	70,746	169,000
Gomel	144,169	144,000	Kopeysk	44,700	149,000
Gorkiy	644,116	876,000	Kostroma	121,205	156,000
Gorlovka	108,693	240,000	Kramatorsk	93,350	117,000
Groznyy	172,468	226,000	Krasnodar	203,946	271,000
Irkutsk	243,380	314,000	Krasnoyarsk	189,999	328,000
Ivanovo	285,069	319,000	Krivoy Rog	197,621	322,000

[a] 1956 data are official estimates, there having been no census since 1939. All cities with a 1956 population of 100,000 or more have been listed, but M.A.'s have been delimited only for Moscow, Leningrad, and Baku (see further statement in Appendix). Names of cities are given as of early 1958; for those recently changed, the former name appears in parentheses; [b] 1956 population including localities subordinate to the city government: 901,000. The city of Sumgait, separated from Baku about 1954, was presumably included in the 1939 census figure, which evidently includes the subordinate localities as of that date; [c] Includes Bezhitsa (1939 pop. 82,331; 1956 pop. 74,000), annexed to Bryansk June 2, 1956. 1956 pop. of Bryansk prior to annexation: 111,000; [d] Not in the U.S.S.R. in January 1939. Dates of populations: Chernovtsy and Kishinev (1/1/1939s), Kaliningrad (5/17/1939); Kaunas (12/31/1939s); [e] In Azerbaydzhan SSR; [f] No 1939 figure located; 1933 official estimate.

[61]

Metropolitan Areas and Principal Cities	Population, Last Census Before 1954	Estimated Population, circa 1955	Metropolitan Areas and Principal Cities	Population, Last Census Before 1954	Estimated Population, circa 1955
U.S.S.R.(cont'd)	(1939)	(1956s)	U.S.S.R.(cont'd)	(1939)	(1956s)
Kurgan	53,224	106,000	Penza	157,145	231,000
Kursk	119,972	179,000	Perm(Molotov)	255,196	538,000
Kutaisi	81,479	114,000	Petropavlovsk[d]	91,678	118,000
Kuybyshev	390,267	760,000	Petrozavodsk	69,728	118,000
Leninakan	67,707	103,000	Poltava	130,305	129,000
LENINGRAD[a] Leningrad	3,600,000 3,015,000	3,500,000 2,819,000	Prokopyevsk	107,227	260,000
Leninsk-Kuznetskiy	81,980	119,000	Riga	393,211[e]	565,000
Lipetsk	66,625	123,000	Rostov-na-Donu	510,253	552,000
Lugansk (Voroshilovgrad)	213,007	251,000	Ryazan	95,358	136,000
Lvov	318,000[b]	387,000	Rybinsk (Shcherbakov)	139,011	162,000
Magnitogorsk	145,870	284,000	Samarkand	134,346	170,000
Makeyevka	240,145	311,000	Saratov	375,860	518,000
Makhachkala	86,847	106,000	Semipalatinsk	109,779	136,000
Minsk	238,772	412,000	Serpukhov	90,766	102,000
Mogilev	99,440	106,000	Sevastopol	111,946	133,000
MOSCOW[c] Moscow	5,600,000 4,137,018	7,300,000 4,839,000	Shakhty	155,081	180,000
Murmansk	117,054	168,000	Simferopol	142,678	159,000
Namangan	77,351	104,000	Smolensk	156,677	131,000
Nikolayev	167,108	206,000	Stalinabad	82,540	191,000
Nizhniy Tagil	159,864	297,000	Stalingrad	445,476	525,000
Novosibirsk	405,589	731,000	Stalino	462,395	625,000
Odessa	604,223	607,000	Stalinogorsk	76,207	109,000
Omsk	280,716	505,000	Stalinsk	169,538	347,000
Ordzhonikidze (Dzaudzhikau)	127,172	159,000	Stavropol[e]	85,100	123,000
Orekhovo-Zuyevo	99,329	109,000	Sverdlovsk	425,544	707,000
Orel	110,567	128,000	Syzran	77,679	169,000
Orenburg(Chkalov)	172,925	226,000	Taganrog	188,808	189,000
Orsk	65,799	157,000	Tallin	144,978[b]	257,000
			Tambov	121,285	150,000

[a] 1956 (and apparently 1939) figures refer to city proper. 1956 population including certain suburban cities and localities cubordinate to the city government: 3,176,000. The 1939 census figure usually published (3,191,304) probably includes some of the places subordinate in 1956. Both M.A. figures are IUR estimates; [b] Not in the U.S.S.R. in January 1939. Dates of populations: Lvov and Tallin (1/1/1939s), Riga (1939s); [c] Both M.A. figures are IUR estimates, and include four suburban cities of more than 100,000: Babushkin (1939: 70,470; 1956: 103,000), Kuntsevo (1939: 60,963; 1956: 111,000), Perovo (1939: 77,727; 1956: 132,000), and Podolsk (1939: 72,422; 1956: 113,000); [d] In Kazakh SSR; [e] In Stavropol oblast, Russian SFSR.

Metropolitan Areas and Principal Cities	Population, Last Census Before 1954	Estimated Population, circa 1955	Metropolitan Areas and Principal Cities	Population, Last Census Before 1954	Estimated Population, circa 1955
U.S.S.R.(cont'd)	(1939)	(1956s)	U.S.S.R.(cont'd)	(1939)	(1956s)
Tashkent	585,005	778,000	Vitebsk	167,424	128,000
Tbilisi	519,175	635,000	Vladimir	66,761	121,000
Tomsk	141,215	224,000	Vladivostok	206,432	265,000
Tula	272,403	320,000	Vologda	95,194	127,000
Tyumen	75,537	125,000	Voronezh	326,836	400,000
Ufa[a]	245,863	471,000	Yaroslavl	298,065	374,000
Ulan-Ude	129,417	158,000	Yerevan	200,031	385,000
Ulyanovsk	102,106	183,000	Zaporozhye	289,188	381,000
Ussuriysk (Voroshilov)	70,628	101,000	Zhdanov	222,427	273,000
Vilnyus	209,000[b]	200,000	Zlatoust	99,272	143,000
Vinnitsa	92,868	105,000			

[a] Includes Chernikovsk (1956 pop. 206,000), which was part of Ufa in 1939, became a separate city in 1944, and was reannexed to Ufa August 24, 1956. 1956 population of Ufa prior to annexation: 265,000; [b] Not in the U.S.S.R. in January 1939. Date of population: (1939s).

APPENDIX | COMPONENT UNITS OF
EACH METROPOLITAN AREA,
WITH SOURCES OF DATA

Section I: AFRICA

ALGERIA

Units: ALGIERS (ALGER): communes of Alger, Birmandreis, Bouzaréa, El-Biar, Hussein-Dey, Kouba, Maison-Carrée, and Saint-Eugène. BÔNE: Bône commune. CONSTANTINE: Constantine commune. ORAN: communes of Mers-el-Kébir and Oran.

Sources: 1948 figures: Algeria, Service de Statistique Générale, *Résultats Statistiques du Dénombrement de la Population effectué le 31 Octobre 1954,* Vol. I (Alger, 1956); for city populations, Statistical Office of the United Nations, Department of Economic and Social Affairs, *Demographic Yearbook, 1955,* 7th issue (New York, 1955). 1954 figures: Algeria, Service de Statistique Générale, *op. cit.*

ANGOLA

Units: LUANDA: Luanda concelho.

Sources: 1950 figures: Angola, Repartição Técnica de Estatística Geral, *II Recenseamento Geral da População, 1950* (Luanda, 1953). 1955 figures: for Luanda, Angola, Repartição Técnica de Estatística Geral, *Boletim Mensal de Estatística,* no. 4 (Luanda, April, 1956); for Lauanda M.A., IUR estimate.

BELGIAN CONGO

Units: ÉLISABETHVILLE: Élisabethville urban area. LÉOPOLD-VILLE: Léopoldville urban area.

Sources: 1953 figures: Official estimates, Belgium, Statistiques et Documentation du Ministère des Colonies, *La Situation Économique du Congo Belge, 1954* (Brussels, 1954). 1955 figures: IUR estimates.

EGYPT

Units: ALEXANDRIA (EL ISKANDERIYA): Alexandria governorate. CAIRO (EL QAHIRA): Cairo governorate and El Giza bandura. EL MAHALLA EL KUBRA: El Mahalla el Kubra bandura. MANSURA: Mansura bandura. PORT SAID: Districts 1–3 and El Mina (including Port Fouad). SUEZ: Suez district. TANTA: Tanta Bandura I and Tanta Bandura II.

Sources: 1947 figures: Egypt, Statistical and Census Department, *Population Census of Egypt, 1947,* "General Tables" (Cairo, 1954). 1955 figures: IUR estimates.

ETHIOPIA AND ERITREA

Units: ADDIS ABABA: Addis Ababa municipality. ASMARA: Asmara municipality.

Sources: 1952 figures: for Addis Ababa, Ethiopia, Ministry of Commerce and Industry, *Economic Progress of Ethiopia, 1955* (Addis Ababa); for Asmara, *ibid.,* estimate, figure not dated. 1955 figures: IUR estimates.

FRENCH WEST AFRICA

Units: ABIDJAN: Abidjan commune. DAKAR: Dakar delegation (comprised of Dakar commune, Gorée commune, and the Banlieue of Dakar).

Sources: 1946 figures: France, Ministère de la France d'Outre-Mer, Service de Statistiques, *Annuaire Statistique de l'Union Française Outre-Mer, 1939–1949* (Paris, 1951); and France, Institut National de la Statistique et des Études Économiques, *Annuaire Statistique de la France, 1956* (Paris). 1955 figures: provisional returns from the 1955 censuses supplied by Direction des Services de la Statistique

Générale et de la Mécanographie de l'Afrique Occidentale Française, Gouvernement Générale de l'Afrique Occidentale Française, Dakar.

GHANA

Units: ACCRA: Accra municipality and Accra administrative district.
Sources: 1948 figures: Gold Coast, Census Commissioner, *The Gold Coast Census of Population, 1948,* "Report and Tables" (London, 1950). 1955 figures: IUR estimates.

KENYA

Units: NAIROBI: Nairobi city.
Sources: 1948 figures and 1955 figures: supplied by the East African Statistical Department, Nairobi, Kenya.

LIBYA

Units: TRIPOLI (TARABULUS): Tripoli city.
Sources: 1936 figures: Istituto Fascista dell'Africa Italiana, *Annuario dell'Africa Italiana, 1938–1939* (Roma, 1939). 1954 figures: Libya, Ministry of National Economy, Department of Census and Statistics, *Preliminary Results of the General Population Census, 1954* (1955).

MADAGASCAR

Units: TANANARIVE (ANTANANARIVO): Tananarive district.
Sources: 1951 figures: Madagascar, Service de Statistique Générale, *Annuaire Statistique de Madagascar,* Vol. I, 1938–1951 (Tananarive, 1953). 1955 figures: IUR estimates.

MOROCCO

Units: TANGIER: composed of the former Tangier International Zone.
Sources: 1951/52 figures: for Tangier M.A., Statistical Office of the United Nations, Department of Economic and Social Affairs, *Demographic Yearbook, 1956* (New York, 1956); for Tangier city, *ibid.,* and IUR estimate; for the other cities, results of the 1951/52 census as quoted by Morocco, Service Central des Statistiques, *La Conjoncture Économique Marocaine, 1953* (Rabat, 1954). 1955 figures: for Casa-

[67]

blanca, official estimate, Cabinet du Gouverneur, Ville de Casablanca; for Tangier M.A., Statistical Office of the United Nations, Department of Economic and Social Affairs, *Demographic Yearbook, 1956* (New York, 1956); for Tangier city, *ibid.,* and IUR estimate; for the other cities, IUR estimates.

NIGERIA

Units: IBADAN: Ibadan city and environs, as reported in census. IFE: Ife town. IWO: Iwo city. KANO: Kano city and township. LAGOS: Lagos township and Ikeja Native Authority. OGBOMOSHO: Ogbomosho town. OSHOGBO: Oshogbo town.

Sources: 1952 figures: Nigeria, Census Superintendent, *Population Census of the Western Region of Nigeria, 1952,* Bulletins 1–9 and "Census Report and Tables" (Lagos); Nigeria, Department of Statistics, *Population Census of the Northern Region of Nigeria, 1952,* Bulletin 8 and "Census Report and Tables" (Lagos, 1952–). 1955 figures: IUR estimates.

RHODESIA AND NYASALAND

Units: BULAWAYO: Bulawayo and suburbs, as reported in the census. SALISBURY: Salisbury and suburbs, as reported in the census.

Sources: 1951 figures: estimates based on Central African Statistical Office, *Census of Population of Southern Rhodesia, 1951* (Salisbury, 1954). The census includes only "natives in employment"; total population estimated by IUR on assumption that this category represents approximately two-thirds of total natives. 1956 figures: estimates based on 1956 census returns as given by Rhodesia and Nyasaland, Federal Information Department, *Towns of Rhodesia & Nyasaland* (Salisbury, 1956). (Total population estimated by IUR by same method as for 1951 data.)

SUDAN

Units: KHARTOUM—OMDURMAN: towns of Burri-el-Lamab, Khartoum, Khartoum North, Omdurman, and Shambat; and Tuti Island.

[68]

Sources: 1953 figures: Sudan, Ministry for Social Affairs, Department of Statistics, *The 1953 Pilot Population Census for the First Population Census in Sudan* (Khartoum, 1955). 1955 figures: Sudan, Ministry for Social Affairs, Population Census Office, *First Population Census of Sudan, 1955–56,* Interim Reports 1–8 (Khartoum, 1957).

TANGANYIKA

Units: DAR-ES-SALAAM: Dar-es-Salaam municipality.

Sources: 1952 figures: *Encylopaedia Britannica World Atlas* (1957). 1957 figures: preliminary results of 1957 census provided by the East African Statistical Department, Nairobi, Kenya.

TUNISIA

Units: TUNIS: communes of L'Ariana, Le Bardo, La Goulette, La Manouba, Maxula-Radès, and Tunis.

Sources: 1946 figures: Tunisia, Service Tunisien des Statistiques, *Annuaire Statistique de la Tunisie, 1940–1946* (Tunis, 1947). 1956 figures: for Tunis city proper, France, Institut National de la Statistique et des Études Économiques, *Annuaire Statistique de la France, 1956* (Paris); for Tunis M.A., IUR estimate.

UNION OF SOUTH AFRICA

Units: BLOEMFONTEIN: Bloemfontein district. CAPE TOWN: districts of Bellville, Cape, Simonstown, and Wynberg. DURBAN: Durban district. EAST LONDON: East London district. JOHANNESBURG: districts of Benoni, Boksburg, Brakpan, Germiston, Johannesburg, Roodepoort, and Springs. PORT ELIZABETH: Port Elizabeth district. PRETORIA: Pretoria district. VEREENIGING—VANDERBIJLPARK: Vereeniging district.

Sources: 1951 figures: Union of South Africa, Department of Census and Statistics, *Population Census, 8th May, 1951* (Pretoria, 1955). 1955 figures: IUR estimates for Dec. 31, 1955 based in part on 1956 estimates for official urban areas, Bureau of Census and Statistics, *Monthly Bulletin of Statistics* (Dec., 1956), and 1955 and 1956 estimates for municipalities in *South African Municipal Year Book, 1956–1957* (Pretoria). The Johannesburg city estimate is from the latter source.

CANADA

Units: CALGARY: Census Division No. 6 of Alberta (1956 and 1951 boundaries differ). EDMONTON: Census Division No. 11 of Alberta (1956 and 1951 boundaries differ). HALIFAX: Halifax county. HAMILTON: counties of Halton and Wentworth. LONDON: Middlesex county. MONTREAL: counties of Chambly, Laprairie, and Montréal & Jésus Islands. OTTAWA: counties of Carleton, Gatineau, and Hull. QUEBEC: counties of Lévis and Québec. TORONTO: counties of Ontario, Peel, and York. VANCOUVER: Census Division No. 4 of British Columbia. VICTORIA: Census Division No. 5 of British Columbia. WINDSOR: Essex county. WINNIPEG: Census Divisions Nos. 5, 6, and 9 of Manitoba.

Sources: 1951 figures: Canada, Dominion Bureau of Statistics, *Census of Canada, 1951,* Vol. I, "Population, General Characteristics," Vol. IV, "Labor Force, Occupations and Industries" (Ottawa, 1953). 1956 figures: Canada, Dominion Bureau of Statistics, *Census of Canada, 1956,* Bulletins 1–2, 1–3, 1–4, and 1–5 (Ottawa, 1957).

UNITED STATES

Units: AKRON, Ohio: Summit county. ALBANY—SCHENECTADY—TROY, N.Y.: counties of Albany, Rensselaer, and Schenectady. ALBUQUERQUE, N.Mex.: Bernalillo county. ALLENTOWN—BETHLEHEM—EASTON, Pa.: counties of Lehigh, Pa., Northampton, Pa., and Warren, N.J. ALTOONA, Pa.: Blair county. ASHEVILLE, N.C.: Buncombe county. ATLANTA, Ga.: counties of Cobb, De Kalb, and Fulton. ATLANTIC CITY, N.J.: Atlantic county. AUGUSTA, Ga.: counties of Richmond, Ga. and Aiken, S.C. AUSTIN, Texas: Travis county. BALTIMORE, Md.: city of Baltimore; counties of Anne Arundel and Baltimore. BATON ROUGE, La.: East Baton Rouge parish. BEAUMONT—PORT ARTHUR, Texas: Jefferson county. BINGHAMTON, N.Y.: Broome county. BIRMINGHAM, Ala.: Jefferson county. BOSTON—LOWELL—LAWRENCE, Mass.: counties of Essex, Middlesex,

Norfolk, and Suffolk. BRIDGEPORT—STAMFORD—NORWALK, Conn.: Fairfield county. BROCKTON, Mass.: Plymouth county. BUFFALO, N.Y.: counties of Erie and Niagara. CANTON, Ohio: Stark county. CEDAR RAPIDS, Iowa: Linn county. CHARLESTON, S.C.: Charleston county. CHARLESTON, W.Va.: counties of Fayette and Kanawha. CHARLOTTE, N.C.: Mecklenburg county. CHATTANOOGA, Tenn.: counties of Hamilton, Tenn., and Walker, Ga. CHICAGO, Ill.: counties of Cook, Ill., Du Page, Ill., Kane, Ill., Lake, Ill., Will, Ill., and Lake, Ind. CINCINNATI, Ohio: counties of Hamilton, Ohio, Campbell, Ky., and Kenton, Ky. CLEVELAND, Ohio: counties of Cuyahoga and Lake. COLUMBIA, S.C.: Richland county. COLUMBUS, Ga.: counties of Chattahoochee, Ga., Muscogee, Ga., and Russell, Ala. COLUMBUS, Ohio: Franklin county. CORPUS CHRISTI, Texas: Nueces county. DALLAS, Texas: Dallas county. DAVENPORT, Iowa—ROCK ISLAND—MOLINE, Ill.: counties of Rock Island, Ill. and Scott, Iowa. DAYTON, Ohio: counties of Greene and Montgomery. DENVER, COLO.: counties of Adams, Arapahoe, Denver, and Jefferson. DES MOINES, Iowa: Polk county. DETROIT, Mich.: counties of Macomb, Oakland, and Wayne. DULUTH, Minn.—SUPERIOR, Wis.: counties of St. Louis, Minn. and Douglas, Wis. DURHAM, N.C.: Durham county. EL PASO, Texas: El Paso county. ERIE, Pa.: Erie county. EVANSVILLE, Ind.: Vanderburgh county. FALL RIVER—NEW BEDFORD, Mass.: Bristol county. FLINT, Mich.: Genesee county. FORT WAYNE, Ind.: Allen county. FORT WORTH, Texas: Tarrant county. FRESNO, Calif.: Fresno county. GALVESTON, Texas: Galveston county. GRAND RAPIDS, Mich.: Kent county. GREENSBORO—HIGH POINT, N.C.: Guilford county. GREENVILLE, S.C.: Greenville county. HAMILTON—MIDDLETOWN, Ohio: Butler county. HARRISBURG, Pa.: counties of Cumberland and Dauphin. HARTFORD—NEW BRITAIN—BRISTOL, Conn.: Hartford county. HOUSTON, Texas: Harris county. HUNTINGTON, W.Va.—ASHLAND, Ky.: counties of Cabell, W.Va., Wayne, W.Va., Boyd, Ky., and Lawrence, Ohio. INDIANAPOLIS, Ind.: Marion county. JACKSON, Mich.: Jackson county. JACKSON, Miss.: Hinds county. JACKSONVILLE, Fla.: Duval county. JOHNSTOWN, Pa.: counties of Cambria and Somerset. KALAMAZOO, Mich.: Kalamazoo county.

KANSAS CITY, Mo.: counties of Clay, Mo., Jackson, Mo., Johnson, Kans., and Wyandotte, Kans. KNOXVILLE, Tenn.: counties of Anderson, Blount, and Knox. LANCASTER, Pa.: Lancaster county. LANSING, Mich.: Ingham county. LEXINGTON, Ky.: Fayette county. LINCOLN, Nebr.: Lancaster county. LITTLE ROCK—NORTH LITTLE ROCK, Ark.: Pulaski county. LORAIN—ELYRIA, Ohio: Lorain county. LOS ANGELES, Calif.: counties of Los Angeles and Orange. LOUISVILLE, Ky.: counties of Jefferson, Ky., Clark, Ind., and Floyd, Ind. LUBBOCK, Texas: Lubbock county. MACON, Ga.: counties of Bibb and Houston. MADISON, Wis.: Dane county. MANCHESTER, N.H.: Hillsborough county. MEMPHIS, Tenn.: Shelby county. MIAMI, Fla.: Dade county. MILWAUKEE, Wis.: Milwaukee county. MINNEAPOLIS—ST. PAUL, Minn.: counties of Anoka, Dakota, Hennepin, and Ramsey. MOBILE, Ala.: Mobile county. MONTGOMERY, Ala.: Montgomery county. NASHVILLE, Tenn.: Davidson county. NEW HAVEN—WATERBURY, Conn.: New Haven county. NEW ORLEANS, La.: parishes of Jefferson, Orleans, and St. Bernard. NEW YORK—NORTHEASTERN NEW JERSEY: New York City, N.Y. (counties of Bronx, Kings, New York, Queens, and Richmond); counties of Nassau, N.Y., Rockland, N.Y., Suffolk, N.Y., Westchester, N.Y., Bergen, N.J., Essex, N.J., Hudson, N.J., Middlesex, N.J., Morris, N.J., Passaic, N.J., Somerset, N.J., and Union, N.J. NORFOLK—PORTSMOUTH, Va.: cities of Norfolk, Portsmouth, and South Norfolk; counties of Norfolk and Princess Anne. OKLAHOMA CITY, Okla.: Oklahoma county. OMAHA, Nebr.: counties of Douglas, Nebr., Sarpy, Nebr., and Pottawattamie, Iowa. ORLANDO, Fla.: Orange county. PEORIA, Ill.: counties of Peoria and Tazewell. PHILADELPHIA, Pa.: counties of Bucks, Pa., Chester, Pa., Delaware, Pa., Montgomery, Pa., Philadelphia, Pa., Burlington, N.J., Camden, N.J., and Gloucester, N.J. PHOENIX, Ariz.: Maricopa county. PITTSBURGH, Pa.: counties of Allegheny, Beaver, Washington, and Westmoreland. PITTSFIELD, Mass.: Berkshire county. PORTLAND, Maine: Cumberland county. PORTLAND, Oregon: counties of Clackamas, Oreg., Multnomah, Oreg., Washington, Oreg., and Clark, Wash. PROVIDENCE, R.I.: counties of Bristol, Kent, and Providence. RACINE, Wis.:

Racine county. RALEIGH, N.C.: Wake county. READING, Pa.: Berks county. RICHMOND, Va.: city of Richmond; counties of Chesterfield and Henrico. ROANOKE, Va.: Roanoke city and county. ROCHESTER, N.Y.: Monroe county. ROCKFORD, Ill.: Winnebago county. SACRAMENTO, Calif.: Sacramento county. SAGINAW, Mich.: Saginaw county. ST. LOUIS, MO.: city of St. Louis, Mo.; counties of St. Charles, Mo., St. Louis, Mo., Madison, Ill., and St. Clair, Ill. SALT LAKE CITY, Utah: Salt Lake county. SAN ANTONIO, Texas: Bexar county. SAN BERNARDINO, Calif.: San Bernardino county. SAN DIEGO, Calif.: San Diego county. SAN FRANCISCO—OAKLAND, Calif.: counties of Alameda, Contra Costa, Marin, San Francisco, San Mateo, and Solano. SAN JOSE, Calif.: Santa Clara county. SAVANNAH, Ga.: Chatham county. SCRANTON, Pa.: Lackawanna county. SEATTLE, Wash.: King county. SHREVEPORT, La.: Caddo parish. SIOUX CITY, Iowa: Woodbury county. SOUTH BEND, Ind.: St. Joseph county. SPOKANE, Wash.: Spokane county. SPRINGFIELD, Ill.: Sangamon county. SPRINGFIELD, Mo.: Greene county. SPRINGFIELD, Ohio: Clark county. SPRING-FIELD—HOLYOKE, Mass.: counties of Hampden and Hampshire. STOCKTON, Calif.: San Joaquin county. SYRACUSE, N.Y.: Onondaga county. TACOMA, Wash.: Pierce county. TAMPA–ST. PETERSBURG, Fla.: counties of Hillsborough and Pinellas. TERRE HAUTE, Ind.: Vigo county. TOLEDO, Ohio: Lucas county. TOPEKA, Kansas: Shawnee county. TRENTON, N.J.: Mercer county. TULSA, Okla.: Tulsa county. UTICA—ROME, N.Y.: counties of Herkimer and Oneida. WACO, Texas: McLennan county. WASHINGTON, D.C.: District of Columbia; cities of Alexandria, Va., and Falls Church, Va.; counties of Montgomery, Md., Prince Georges, Md., Arlington, Va., and Fairfax, Va. WATERLOO, Iowa: Black Hawk county. WHEELING, W.Va.—STEUBENVILLE, Ohio: counties of Brooke, W.Va., Hancock, W.Va., Marshall, W.Va., Ohio, W.Va., Belmont, Ohio, and Jefferson, Ohio. WICHITA, Kans.: Sedgwick county. WILKES-BARRE—HAZLETON, Pa.: Luzerne county. WILMINGTON, Del.: counties of New Castle, Del. and Salem, N.J. WINSTON-SALEM, N.C.: Forsyth county. WORCESTER, Mass.: Worcester county.

York, Pa.: York county. Youngstown, Ohio: counties of Mahoning, Ohio, Trumbull, Ohio, and Mercer, Pa.

Sources: 1950 figures: Donald J. Bogue, *Population Growth in Standard Metropolitan Areas, 1900–1950* (Washington, D.C.: Housing and Home Finance Agency, 1953). 1956 figures: estimates provided through the courtesy of Rand McNally & Company. Most of these estimates appear in the Rand McNally *Commercial Atlas and Marketing Guide, 1958* (Chicago, 1958).

Section III: AMERICA, MIDDLE

COSTA RICA

Units: San José: cantones of Central, Goicoechea, Montes de Oca, Moravia, and Tibás.

Sources: 1950 figures: Costa Rica, Dirección General de Estadística y Censos, *Censo de Población de Costa Rica, 22 de Mayo de 1950* (San José, 1953). 1955 figures: Costa Rica, Dirección General de Estadística y Censos, *Algunas Características Demográficas del Área Metropolitana de San José* (San José, 1957).

CUBA

Units: Camagüey: Camagüey city. Havana (La Habana): municipios of Bauta, Guanabacoa, Habana, Marianao, Regla, Santa María del Rosario, and Santiago de las Vegas. Santiago de Cuba: Santiago de Cuba municipio.

Sources: 1953 figures: Cuba, Oficina Nacional de los Censos Demográfico y Electoral, *Censos de Población, Viviendas y Electoral, Enero 28 de 1953, Informe General* (Havana, 1955). 1955 figures: IUR estimates.

DOMINICAN REPUBLIC

Units: Ciudad Trujillo: Santo Domingo distrito.

Sources: 1950 figures: Dominican Republic, Dirección General de Estadística, *Población de la República Dominicana Censada en 1950* (Ciudad Trujillo, 1954). 1955 figures: IUR estimates.

[74]

EL SALVADOR

Units: SAN SALVADOR: San Salvador distrito.
Sources: 1950 figures: El Salvador, Dirección General de Estadística y Censos, *Segundo Censo de Población, 13 Junio 1950* (San Salvador, 1954). 1956 figures: for San Salvador city, official estimate, El Salvador, Dirección General de Estadística y Censos; for San Salvador M.A., IUR estimate.

GUATEMALA

Units: GUATEMALA CITY: Guatemala municipio.
Sources: 1950 figures: Guatemala, Dirección General de Estadística, *Sexto Censo de Población* (Guatemala City, 1957). 1955 figures: IUR estimates.

HAITI

Units: PORT-AU-PRINCE: communes of Pétionville and Port-au-Prince.
Sources: 1950 figures: U.S. Dept. of Commerce, Business Information Service, *1950 Census of the Americas, Population Census—Urban Area Data, No. 5—Haiti* (Washington, 1954). 1955 figures: IUR estimates.

HONDURAS

Units: TEGUCIGALPA: Distrito Central municipio.
Sources: 1950 figures: Honduras, Dirección General de Estadística, *Resumen General del Censo de Población 18 Junio 1950* (Tegucigalpa, 1952). 1955 figures: IUR estimates.

MEXICO

Units: AGUASCALIENTES: Aguascalientes municipio. CHIHUAHUA: Chihuahua municipio. CIUDAD JUÁREZ: Juárez municipio. GUADALAJARA: municipios of Guadalajara and Tlaquepaque. LEÓN: León municipio. MÉRIDA: Mérida municipio. MEXICO CITY: in the Distrito Federal, delegaciones of Mexico City, Atzcapotzalco, Coyoacán, Gustavo A. Madero, Ixtacalco, Ixtapalapa, and Obregón; in the state of Mexico, municipios of Naucalpan and Tlalnepantla. MONTERREY: municipios of Garza García, Guadalupe, Monterrey, and San Nicolás de los Garzas. PUEBLA: Municipios of Cuantlancingo, Puebla, San Felipe Hueyotlipan, and San Jer-

ónimo Caleras. SAN LUIS POTOSÍ: San Luis Potosí municipio.
TAMPICO: municipios of Ciudad Madero and Tampico.
TORREÓN—GÓMEZ PALACIO: municipios of Gómez Palacio
and Torreón. VERACRUZ: municipios of Boca del Río and
Veracruz.

Sources: 1950 figures: Mexico, Dirección General de Estadística, *Séptimo Censo General de Población 6 de Junio
de 1950* (México, D.F., 1952–), appropriate state volumes.
1955 figures: IUR estimates.

NICARAGUA

Units: MANAGUA: Managua municipio.
Sources: 1950 figures: Nicaragua, Dirección General de Estadística y Censos, *Censo General de Población de la República de Nicaragua 1950,* Vol. X, "Informe General y Cifras
del Departamento de Managua" (Managua, 1951). 1955
figures: IUR estimates.

PANAMA

Units: PANAMA CITY: Panamá distrito.
Sources: 1950 figures: Panama, Dirección de Estadística y
Censo, *Quinto Censo de Población,* Vol. V, "Población
Urbana" (Panamá, 1956). 1955 figures: IUR estimates.

PUERTO RICO

Units: PONCE: Ponce municipio. SAN JUAN: municipios of
Bayamón, Cataño, Guaynabo, Río Piedras (annexed to San
Juan in 1951), and San Juan.
Sources: 1950 figures: U.S. Bureau of the Census, *United
States Census of Population, 1950,* Vol. II, part 53 (Wash-
ington, 1952). 1955 figures: IUR estimates.

WEST INDIES, BRITISH

Units: KINGSTON: parishes of Kingston and St. Andrew. PORT-
OF-SPAIN: city of Port-of-Spain; wards of Diego Martin and
St. Ann's.
Sources: 1946 figures: Jamaica, Central Bureau of Statistics,
West Indian Census, part G, "Census of the Colony of
Trinidad and Tobago, 9th April, 1946" (taken by the West
Indian Census Office) (Kingston, 1950). 1953 figures: Ja-

maica, Central Bureau of Statistics, *Sample Survey of Population Kingston Metropolitan Area, 1953* (Kingston, 1954). 1955 figures: for Kingston city and M.A., Jamaica, Central Bureau of Statistics, *1956 Report on Jamaica* (Kingston, 1957); for Port-of-Spain city, estimate by the Central Statistical Office of Trinidad; for Port-of-Spain M.A., IUR estimate.

Section IV: AMERICA, SOUTH

ARGENTINA

Units: BAHÍA BLANCA: Bahía Blanca departamento. BUENOS AIRES: city of Buenos Aires; partidos of Almirante Brown, Avellaneda, Esteban Echeverría, Florencio Varela, General San Martín, General Sarmiento, La Matanza, Lanús, Lomas de Zamora, Merlo, Moreno, Morón, Quilmes, San Fernando, San Isidro, Tigre, and Vicente López. CÓRDOBA: Capital (Córdoba) departamento. LA PLATA: La Plata departamento. MAR DEL PLATA: General Pueyrredón departamento. MENDOZA: departamentos of Capital (Mendoza), Godoy Cruz, and Guaymallén. PARANÁ: Paraná departamento. ROSARIO: Rosario departamento. SAN JUAN: departamentos of Rawson, San Juan, and Santa Lucía. SANTA FE: La Capital (Santa Fe) departamento. TUCUMÁN: Capital (Tucumán) departamento.
Sources: 1947 figures: Argentina, Dirección Nacional de Estadística y Censos, *VI Censo General de la Nación,* Vol. I, "Censo de Población" (Buenos Aires, 1957). 1955 figures: IUR estimates.

BOLIVIA

Units: LA PAZ: Murillo provincia.
Sources: 1950 figures: Bolivia, Dirección Nacional de Estadística y Censos, *Censo de Población de la República de Bolivia, 5 de Septiembre de 1950* (La Paz, 1951). Note: The figures presented are officially corrected for underenumeration. 1955 figures: IUR estimates.

[77]

BRAZIL

Units: BELÉM: Belém município. BELO HORIZONTE: Belo Horizonte município. CAMPINAS: Campinas município. CURITIBA: Curitiba municipio. FORTALEZA: Fortaleza município. JOÃO PESSOA: João Pessoa município. JUIZ DE FORA: Juiz de Fora município. MACEIÓ: Maceió município. NATAL: Natal município. PÔRTO ALEGRE: municípios of Canoas and Pôrto Alegre. RECIFE: municípios of Jaboatão, Olinda, Paulista, and Recife. RIO DE JANEIRO: Distrito Federal; municípios of Duque de Caxias, Nilópolis, Niterói, Nova Iguaçu, São Gonçalo, and São João de Meriti. SALVADOR: Salvador município. SANTOS: municípios of Guarujá, Santos, and São Vicente. SÃO LUÍS: São Luís município. SÃO PAULO: municípios of Guarulhos, Santo André, São Bernardo do Campo, São Caetano do Sul, and São Paulo.

Sources: 1950 figures: Brazil, Instituto Brasileiro de Geográfia e Estatística, Conselho Nacional de Estatística, Serviço Nacional de Recenseamento, *VI Recenseamento do Brasil: Censo Demográfico (1 de Julho de 1950)* (Rio de Janeiro, 1951–1953), appropriate state volumes. 1955 figures: IUR estimates.

BRITISH GUIANA

Units: GEORGETOWN: Georgetown municipal area and environs.

Sources: 1946 figures: Jamaica, Central Bureau of Statistics, *West Indian Census, 1946* (taken by the West Indian Census Office), "Census of the Colony of British Guiana, 9th April, 1946" (Kingston, 1950). 1956 figures: IUR estimates.

CHILE

Units: CONCEPCIÓN—TALCAHUANO: comunas of Concepción, Penco, and Talcahuano. SANTIAGO: comunas of Barrancas, Cisterna, Conchalí, La Granja, Las Condes, Ñuñoa, Providencia, Puente Alto, Quinta Normal, Renca, San Miguel, and Santiago. VALPARAÍSO: comunas of Valparaíso and Viña del Mar.

Sources: 1952 figures: Chile, Dirección General de Estadística, *XII Censo General de Población y de Vivienda, 24 de Abril de 1952,* Vol. I, "Resumen del País" (Santiago, 1956). 1955 figures: IUR estimates.

COLOMBIA

Units: BARRANQUILLA: municipios of Barranquilla, Puerto Colombia, and Soledad. BOGOTÁ: municipios of Bogotá, Bosa, Engativá, Fontibón, Suba, Usaquén, and Usme. BUCARAMANGA: Bucaramanga municipio. CALI: Cali municipio. CARTAGENA: Cartagena municipio. MANIZALES: Manizales municipio. MEDELLÍN: municipios of Bello, Envigado, Itagüí, and Medellín. PEREIRA: Pereira municipio.

Sources: 1951 figures: Colombia, Departamento Administrativo Nacional de Estadística, *Censo de Población, 9 de Mayo de 1951* (Bogotá, 1954). 1955 figures: IUR estimates.

ECUADOR

Units: GUAYAQUIL: Guayaquil parroquia urbana. QUITO: Quito parroquia urbana.

Sources: 1950 figures: Ecuador, Dirección General de Estadística y Censos, *Información Censal* (Quito, 1951). 1955 figures: IUR estimates.

PARAGUAY

Units: ASUNCIÓN: Asunción departamento.

Sources: 1950 figures: Paraguay, Dirección General de Estadístico y Censos, *Anuario Estadístico, 1948–1953* (Asunción). 1955 figures: IUR estimates.

PERU

Units: AREQUIPA: Arequipa provincia. LIMA: provincias of Callao and Lima.

Sources: 1940 figures: Peru, Dirección Nacional de Estadística, *Censo Nacional de Población de 1940,* Vol. I, "Resumenes Generales" (Lima, 1944). 1955 figures: estimates by the Dirección Nacional de Estadística, Lima.

URUGUAY

Units: MONTEVIDEO: Montevideo departamento.

Sources: Montevideo, Dirección de Censo, Estadística y Registro del Estado Civil, *Boletín Censo y Estadística* (Montevideo, July–Aug., 1950). 1955 figures: *ibid.*, (July–Aug., 1955).

[79]

VENEZUELA

Units: BARQUISIMETO: municipios of Catedral and Concepción. CARACAS: Distrito Federal and Sucre distrito (Miranda). MARACAIBO: municipios of Bolívar, Cacique Mara, Chiquinquirá, Coquibacoa, Cristo de Aranza, Santa Bárbara, and Santa Lucía. VALENCIA: municipios of Candelaria, Catedral, El Socorro, Naguanagua, San Blas, San José, and Santa Rosa.

Sources: 1950 figures: Venezuela, Dirección General de Estadística y Censos Nacionales, *Octavo Censo General de Población (26 de Noviembre de 1950)*, XII, "Resumen General de la República, parte A, Población" (Caracas, 1957). 1955 figures: IUR estimates.

Section V: ASIA

ADEN COLONY

Units: ADEN: Aden Colony (excluding Perim Island).
Sources: 1946 figures: Leon E. Seltzer (ed.), *Columbia Lippincott Gazetteer of the World* (New York, Columbia University Press, 1952). 1955 figures: Aden, District Commissioner, *Aden Colony Census Report, 1955* (n.d.)

AFGHANISTAN

Sources: 1953 figures and 1955 figures: IUR estimates.

BURMA

Sources: 1953 figures: Burma, Census Department, *Advance Publications—1953 Census Stage,* "Advance Releases," Nos. 1–4 (Rangoon). 1955 figures: IUR estimates.

CAMBODIA

Sources: 1950 figure: *Annuaire Statistique du Cambodge, 1952* as cited in Mitchell C. Zadrozny (ed.), *Area Handbook on Cambodia* (Chicago: University of Chicago Press, 1955). 1955 figure: IUR estimate.

CEYLON

Units: COLOMBO: Colombo municipality and the D.R.O. divisions of Mudaliyar and Salpiti Korale.

Sources: 1953 figures: Ceylon, Department of Census and Statistics, *Census of Ceylon, 1953,* Vol. I, "General Report" (Colombo). 1955 figures: IUR estimates.

CHINA: MAINLAND

Note: Cities are listed under their official names as of early 1958, with a few exceptions (such as Tientsin, Swatow) that are rarely known in English by their official names. However, alternate names have been included to aid in identification in the many instances where the official name has been changed since 1945, and to include variant spellings.

Sources: 1922–1949 figures: Leon E. Seltzer (ed.), *Columbia Lippincott Gazetteer of the World* (New York: Columbia University Press, 1952). The 1953 census was China's first, and few of the various earlier figures for cities seem to have had much accuracy. Comparison of the old figure with the new for any given city will usually cast less light on the city's recent growth than on the degree to which previous estimates of its size were in error. 1953 figures: compiled and made available to IUR by Theodore Shabad, whose principal sources were A. G. Shiger, *Administrativno-territorialnoye deleniye zarubezhnykh stran,* second revised edition (Moskva, 1957), who gives as his source for Chinese figures "materials of the 1953 population census"; *Bolshaya Sovetskaya Entsiklopediya,* second edition (Moskva, 1950–); Akademiya Nauk SSSR, Institut Geografii, *Vostochnyy Kitay* (Moskva, 1955); and L.S. Gingold and others, *Ekonomicheskaya Geografiya Kitaya* (Moskva, 1957), which contains maps classifying Chinese cities according to their 1953 population size-groups. There is some conflict between these sources as to the population of Dairen proper; the figure 766,400 is also quoted, and it has not been possible to determine definitely which is the correct one. No specific 1953 populations were located for three cities that appear to have more than 100,000 population (according to the maps in the last-named source); the populations listed for these cities are designated as IUR estimates.

CHINA: TAIWAN

Sources: 1953 figures: official estimates quoted in Arthur F. Raper, *et al., Urban and Industrial Taiwan—Crowded and Resourceful* (Taipei: Foreign Operations Administration, Mutual Security Mission to China and National Taiwan University, 1954). 1955 figures: China Publishing Co., *China Handbook, 1956–57* (Taipei, 1956); and IUR estimates.

HONG KONG

Units: HONG KONG: entire Colony of Hong Kong.
Sources: 1931 figures: Hong Kong, Census Office, *Report on the Census of Hong Kong Taken on the Night of March 7, 1931* (Hong Kong: Noronha and Co., n.d.). 1956 figures: United Kingdom, Colonial Office, *Hong Kong Annual Report, 1956* (Hong Kong, 1957).

INDIA

Units: (Note: "City" in the following list refers to places so described in the Census of India, which include adjacent cantonments, etc., in addition to the municipality proper.) AGRA: Agra City. AHMEDABAD: Ahmedabad City taluka. AJMER: Ajmer municipality. ALIGARH: Aligarh municipality. ALLAHABAD: Allahabad City. ALLEPPEY: Alleppey municipality. AMRAVATI: Amravati City. AMRITSAR: Amritsar City. BANARAS (VARANASI): Banaras City. BANGALORE: Bangalore corporation and Bangalore North taluk. BAREILLY: Bareilly City. BARODA: Baroda municipality. BHAGALPUR: Bhagalpur municipality. BHAVNAGAR: Bhavnagar municipality. BHOPAL: Bhopal municipality. BIKANER: Bikaner City. BOMBAY: municipality of Bombay (Greater Bombay); talukas of Borivali, Kalyan, and Thana. CALCUTTA: Calcutta district; in Hooghly district, police stations of Bhadreswar, Chinsurah, Serampur, and Uttarpara; in Howrah district, Howrah city, police stations of Bally, Bauria, Jagacha, Sankrail, and Sibpur (outside Howrah city); in 24-Parganas District, police stations of Baranagar, Barrackpur, Behala, Bijpur, Budge-Budge, Dum Dum, Jagaddal, Khardah, Maheshtala, Metiabruz,

Naihati, Noapara, Titagarh, and Tollyganj. COIMBATORE: Coimbatore municipality. CUTTACK: Cuttack municipality. DEHRA DUN: Dehra Dun City. DELHI: Delhi, New Delhi, and the remainder of Delhi State. GAYA: Gaya municipality. GORAKHPUR: Gorakhpur City. GUNTUR: Guntur municipality. GWALIOR: Gwalior City. HUBLI: Hubli municipality. HYDERABAD: Hyderabad City. INDORE: Indore municipality. JABALPUR (JUBBULPORE): Jabalpur City. JAIPUR: Jaipur municipality. JAMNAGAR: Jamnagar municipality. JAMSHEDPUR: Jamshedpur City. JHANSI: Jhansi City. JODHPUR: Jodhpur municipality. JULLUNDUR: Jullundur municipality. KANPUR (CAWNPORE): Kanpur City. KHARAGPUR: Kharagpur town. KOLAR GOLD FIELDS: Kolar Gold Fields municipality. KOLHAPUR: Kolhapur municipality. KOZHIKODE (CALICUT): Kozhikode municipality. LUCKNOW: Lucknow City. LUDHIANA: Ludhiana municipality. MADRAS: Madras corporation and Saidapet taluk. MADURAI (MADURA): Madurai municipality. MANGALORE: Mangalore municipality. MATHURA (MUTTRA): Mathura City. MEERUT: Meerut City. MORADABAD: Moradabad City. MYSORE: Mysore municipality. NAGPUR: Nagpur corporation. PATNA: Patna City. POONA: Poona City taluka. RAJAHMUNDRY: Rajahmundry municipality. RAJKOT: Rajkot municipality. RAMPUR: Rampur municipality. RANCHI: Ranchi City. SAHARANPUR: Saharanpur City. SALEM: Salem municipality. SHAHJAHANPUR: Shahjahanpur City. SHOLAPUR: Sholapur City. SURAT: Surat municipality. TANJORE: Tanjore municipality. TIRUCHIRAPALLI (TRICHINOPOLY): Tiruchirapalli municipality. TIRUNELVELI—PALAYAMCOTTAI (TINNEVELLY—PALAMCOTTAH): municipalities of Palayamcottai and Tirunelveli. TRIVANDRUM: Trivandrum corporation. UJJAIN: Ujjain municipality. VELLORE: Vellore municipality. VIJAYAVADA (BEZWADA): Vijayavada municipality. VISAKHAPATNAM (VIZAGAPATAM): Visakhapatnam municipality. WARANGAL: Warangal City.

Sources: 1951 figures: India, Registrar General, *Census of India, 1951,* Vol. I, "India" and provincial volumes (places of publication and publication dates vary). 1955 figures: IUR estimates.

[83]

INDONESIA

Sources: 1930 figures: Netherlands, Department van Kolon-iën, *Indisch Verslag* (Batavia, 1940). 1955 and 1956 figures: official estimates reported in *Petermanns Geographische Mitteilungen,* Vol. 100, no. 4 (1956).

IRAN

Source: 1956 figures: Iran, Department of Statistics, Ministry of Interior, preliminary results of the 1956 census.

IRAQ

Units: BAGHDAD: city of Baghdad; nahiyas of Adhamiyah and Karradah Sharqiya. BASRA: city of Basra; nahiyas of Hartha and Zubair. MOSUL: Mosul city.
Sources: 1947 figures: Iraq, Directorate General of Census, *Census of Iraq, 1947,* Vols. I–III (Baghdad, 1954). 1955 figures: IUR estimates.

ISRAEL

Units: HAIFA: geographical regions of Haifa Bay and Mount Carmel. JERUSALEM (YERUSHALAYIM): geographical regions of Jerusalem Town and Judean Hills. TEL AVIV-JAFFA (TEL AVIV-YAFO): Yarkon geographical region.
Sources: 1951 figures: Israel, Central Bureau of Statistics and Economic Research, *Statistical Abstract of Israel, 1950–1951* (Jerusalem). 1955 figures: official estimates for December 31, 1955, Israel, Central Bureau of Statistics.

JAPAN

Units: AKITA: Akita-shi. AOMORI: Aomori-shi. ASAHIGAWA: Asahigawa-shi. ASHIKAGA: Ashikaga-shi. FUKUI: Fukui-shi. FUKUOKA: Fukuoka-shi, Kasuga-machi, Ono-machi, Sasa-guri-machi, Shime-machi, Sue-machi, Umi-machi, Wajiro-machi. GIFU—ICHINOMIYA: in Gifu prefecture, Gifu-shi, Kasamatsu-cho, Kitagata-cho, Naka-cho, and Yanaizu-mura; in Aichi prefecture, Bisai-shi, Ichinomiya-shi, and Kisogawa-cho. HACHINOE: Hachinoe-shi. HAKODATE: Hako-date-shi. HAMAMATSU: Hamamatsu-shi and Kami-mura. HIMEJI: Himeji-shi, Kitahama-mura, Matogata-mura, and Oshio-cho. HIROSAKI: Hirosaki-shi. HIROSHIMA—KURE:

Hiroshima-shi, Kure-shi, Fuchu-cho, Funakoshi-cho, Gion-cho, Kaitaichi-cho, Nukushima-son, Saka-cho, Tenno-cho, Yano-cho, and Yasufuruichi-cho. KAGOSHIMA: Kagoshima-shi. KANAZAWA: Kanazawa-shi. KIRYU: in Gumma prefecture, Kiryu-shi, Morita-mura, and Omama-machi; in Tochigi prefecture, Hishi-mura and Sakanishi-machi. KOCHI: Kochi-shi. KOFU: Kofu-shi. KUMAMOTO: Kumamoto-shi. KURASHIKI: Kojima-shi and Kurashiki-shi. KURUME: Kurume-shi. KYOTO: in Kyoto prefecture, Kyoto-shi, Uji-shi, Yawata-cho, and Yodo-cho; in Shiga prefecture, Otsu-shi. MAEBASHI—TAKASAKI: Maebashi-shi and Takasaki-shi. MATSUYAMA: Matsuyama-shi. MIYAZAKI: Miyazaki-shi. MORIOKA: Morioka-shi. MURORAN: Muroran-shi and Horo-betsu-cho. NAGANO: Nagano-shi. NAGAOKA: Nagaoka-shi. NAGASAKI: Nagasaki-shi, Iojima-mura, Koyagi-mura, and Takashima-machi. NAGOYA: Kasugai-shi, Moriyama-shi, Nagoya-shi, Arimatsu-cho, Narumi-cho, Nishibiwajima-cho, Odaka-cho, and Shinkawa-cho. NARA: Nara-shi. NIIGATA: Niigata-shi. NIIHAMA: Niihama-shi, Saijo-shi, and Sumino-cho. NOBEOKA: Nobeoka-shi. NUMAZU—MISHIMA: Mishima-shi, Numazu-shi, Hara-machi, Izunagaoka-cho, and Shimizu-mura. ODAWARA: Odawara-shi. OITA—BEPPU: Beppu-shi and Oita-shi. OKAYAMA: Okayama-shi. OKAZAKI: Okazaki-shi. OMUDA: in Fukuoka prefecture, Omuda-shi; in Kumamoto prefecture, Arao-shi. ONOMICHI—MIHARA: Mihara-shi and Onomichi-shi. OSAKA—KOBE: in Osaka prefecture, Fuse-shi, Hirakata-shi, Hiraoka-shi, Ibaraki-shi, Ikeda-shi, Izumiotsu-shi, Izumisano-shi, Kaizuka-shi, Ka-wachi-shi, Kawachinagano-shi, Kishiwada-shi, Matsubara-shi, Moriguchi-shi, Neyagawa-shi, Osaka-shi, Sakai-shi, Suita-shi, Takatsuki-shi, Tondabayashi-shi, Toyonaka-shi, Yao-shi, Fujidera-cho, Fukuizumi-cho, Furuichi-cho, Hanyu-mura, Hikisho-cho, Izumi-cho, Kadoma-cho, Kashihara-cho, Kitamatsuo-mura, Kokubu-cho, Mashita-cho, Minoo-cho, Miyake-mura, Mizumoto-mura, Nango-son, Nishishindachi-cho, Nishitottori-mura, Niwakubo-cho, Owada-mura, Ozaki-cho, Shijo-cho, Shijonawate-cho, Shiki-mura, Shimamoto-cho, Shinoda-mura, Shinomiya-mura, Suminodo-cho, Tadaoka-cho, Tajiri-cho, Takaishi-cho, Takawashi-cho, Tarui-cho, Tomioka-cho, Tondacho, Yamada-mura, Yasaka-cho; in Nara prefecture, Ikagura-cho, Oji-cho, Sango-mura; in Hyogo prefecture, Akashi-shi, Amagasaki-shi, Ashiya-shi, Itami-shi, Kakogawa-shi, Kawanishi-shi, Kobe-shi, Nishinomiya-shi, Takarazuka-shi, Takasago-shi, and Ae-mura. OTARU: Otaru-shi. SAGA: Saga-shi. SAPPORO: Sapporo-shi. SASEBO: Sasebo-shi, Kosaza-cho, Sasa-cho, Sechibaru-cho, and Yoshii-cho. SENDAI: Sendai-shi. SHIZUOKA—SHIMIZU: Shimizu-shi, Shizuoka-shi, and Sodeshi-cho. TAKAMATSU: Takamatsu-shi and Busho-zan-cho. TAKAOKA: Shimminato-shi and Takaoka-shi. TOKUSHIMA: Tokushima-shi. TOKUYAMA—KUDAMATSU: Hikari-shi, Kudamatsu-shi, Tokuyama-shi, and Nanyo-machi. TOKYO—YOKOHAMA: in Tokyo prefecture, ward area of Tokyo-to, Akishima-shi, Chofu-shi, Fuchu-shi, Hachioji-shi, Mitaka-shi, Musashino-shi, Ome-shi, Tachi-kawa-shi, Asakawa-machi, Fussa-machi, Higashimurayama-machi, Hino-machi, Hoya-machi, Kiyose-machi, Kodaira-machi, Koganei-machi, Kokubunji-machi, Komae-machi, Kunitachi-machi, Machida-machi, Nishitama-mura, Oku-tama-machi, Tanashi-machi, and Yamato-machi; in Kana-gawa prefecture, Chigasaki-shi, Fujisawa-shi, Hiratsuka-shi, Kamakura-shi, Kawasaki-shi, Yokohama-shi, Yokosuka-shi, Zushi-shi, Hayama-machi, and Oiso-machi; in Chiba prefecture, Chiba-shi, Funabashi-shi, Ichikawa-shi, Mat-sudo-shi, Narashino-shi, Minamigyotoku-machi, and Ura-yasu-machi; in Saitama prefecture, Kawaguchi-shi, Omiya-shi, Urawa-shi, Adachi-machi, Asaka-machi, Toda-machi, Warabi-machi, and Yono-machi. TOYAMA: Namerikawa-shi and Toyama-shi. TOYOHASHI: Toyohashi-shi and Toyo-kawa-shi. UBE—ONODA: Onoda-shi and Ube-shi. UTSUNO-MIYA: Utsunomiya-shi. WAKAYAMA: Kainan-shi and Waka-yama-shi. YAHATA—SHIMONOSEKI—KOKURA: in Fukuoka prefecture, Iizuka-shi, Kokura-shi, Moji-shi, Naogata-shi, Takawa-shi, Tobata-shi, Wakamatsu-shi, Yahata-shi, Ya-mada-shi, Akaide-machi, Ashiya-machi, Chinzei-mura, Futase-machi, Hojo-mura, Honami-mura, Inatsuki-machi, Itoda-machi, Kaho-machi, Kaita-mura, Kanada-machi, Kawara-machi, Kawasaki-machi, Keisen-machi, Kobukuro-machi, Kotake-machi, Kurate-machi, Magarikane-mura, Miyata-machi, Mizumaki-machi, Nakama-machi, Onga-

mura, Shonai-mura, and Usui-machi; in Yamaguchi prefecture, Shimonoseki-shi. YAMAGATA: Yamagata-shi. YOK-
KAICHI: Yokkaichi-shi and Kusu-cho. YOSHIWARA—FUJI-
NOMIYA: Fujinomiya-shi, Yoshiwara-shi, Fujikawa-cho, and
Takaoka-cho.
Sources: 1950 figures: Japan, Bureau of Statistics, Office of
the Prime Minister, *Population Census of 1950,* Vol. VII,
parts 1–46 (Tokyo, 1951–1954). Population for 1950 is
adjusted to 1955 administrative boundaries. 1955 figures:
Japan, Bureau of Statistics, Office of the Prime Minister,
1955 Population Census of Japan, Vol. I (Tokyo, 1956).

JORDAN

Units: AMMAN: Amman city. JERUSALEM (EL QUDS): section
of Jerusalem city in Jordan.
Sources: 1952 figures: Jordan, Department of Statistics, Ministry of Economics, *Housing Census of 1952* (Jerusalem,
n.d.). 1955 figures: IUR estimates.

KASHMIR (JAMMU AND)

Units: SRINAGAR: Srinagar municipality.
Sources: India, Census Commissioner, *Census of India, 1941,*
Vol. XXII (Jammu and Kashmir), parts i and ii, "Essay
and Tables." 1955 figures: IUR estimates.

KOREA, NORTH

Sources: 1944 figures: U.S. Department of State, Office of
Intelligence Research, "Population, Industries and Geographical Setting of Certain Urban Settlements in Korea,"
(DFR Information Paper no. 392, January 9, 1951). 1955
figures: IUR estimates.

KOREA, SOUTH

Sources: 1949 figures: Republic of Korea, Office of Public
Information, Bureau of Statistics, *Statistical Summation,
May, 1949* (Seoul, 1949). 1955 figures: Republic of Korea,
Ministry of Home Affairs, Bureau of Statistics, *First Report
on the Results of the Population Census of August 31,
1955* (Seoul, 1955).

[87]

KUWAIT

Units: KUWAIT: Kuwait city and Suburban Areas "B" and "W."

Sources: 1950 figures: IUR estimates. 1957 figures: Kuwait, Ministry of Social Affairs, *Enumeration of the Inhabitants of Kuwait for the Year 1957* (n.d.).

LEBANON

Sources: 1950 figures: Lebanon, Service de Statistique Générale, Ministère de l'Économie Nationale, *Bulletin Statistique Trimestriel,* Première Trimestre 1951. 1954 figures: Charles W. Churchill, *The City of Beirut: A Socio-Economic Survey* (Beirut, Economic Research Institute of the American University of Beirut.) (Differences in figures may be due partly to differences in coverage.)

MACAU

Units: MACAU: Macau city and the remainder of Macau "overseas province."

Sources: 1950 figures: Macau, Repartição Central dos Serviços de Administração Civil, Secção de Estatística, *Anuário Estatístico de Macau, 1955* (Macau, 1956). 1955 figures: for Macau M.A., Statistical Office of the United Nations, Department of Economic and Social Affairs, *Demographic Yearbook, 1956* (New York, 1956); for Macau city, IUR estimate.

MALAYA

Units: GEORGE TOWN: George Town municipality, mukim 16 of Penang (portion outside the limits of George Town municipality), mukim 18 of Penang (portion outside the limits of George Town municipality), and mukims 14 and 15 (including the town of Butterworth) in the Northern District of Province Wellesley. IPOH: towns of Ipoh and Meglembu; Ulukinta mukim (portion outside the limits of Ipoh town and Meglembu town). KUALA LUMPUR: municipality of Kuala Lumpur; mukims of Ampang, Batu, and Kuala Lumpur (portion outside the limits of Kuala Lumpur municipality.)

Sources: 1947 figures: M.V. del Tufo, *Malaya: A Report on the 1947 Census of Population* (London: Crown Agents for the Colonies, n.d.). 1955 figures: IUR estimates.

NEPAL

Units: KATHMANDU—LALITPUR: cities of Kathmandu and Lalitpur (Patan).

Sources: 1952–1954 figures: census data from communication, Census Director, Department of Statistics, Government of Nepal, Kathmandu, Nepal. 1955 figures: IUR estimates.

PAKISTAN

Units: CHITTAGONG: Chittagong municipality and the remainder of Greater Chittagong City. DACCA: Dacca municipality and the remainder of Greater Dacca City. GUJRANWALA: Gujranwala municipality. HYDERABAD: Hyderabad municipality and cantonment. KARACHI: Karachi municipality and the remainder of the Federal Capital Area. LAHORE: Lahore municipality and cantonment. LYALLPUR: Lyallpur municipality. MULTAN: Multan municipality and cantonment. PESHAWAR: Peshawar municipality and cantonment. RAWALPINDI: Rawalpindi municipality. SIALKOT: Sialkot municipality and cantonment.

Sources: 1951 figures: Pakistan, Office of the Census Commissioner, *Census of Pakistan, 1951* (Karachi, 1951–). 1955 figures: IUR estimates.

PHILIPPINES

Units: CEBU: city of Cebu; municipalities of Consolacion, Mandaue, and Talisay. ILOILO: Iloilo city. MANILA: cities of Cavite, Manila, Quezon City, and Rizal (formerly Pasay municipality); municipalities of Angono, Bacoor, Cainta, Caloocan, Makati, Malabon, Mandaluyong, Marikina, Meycauayan, Navotas, Obando, Paranaque, Pasig, Pateros, Polo, San Juan del Monte, Tagig, Taytay, and Teresa.

Sources: 1948 figures: Philippines, Bureau of the Census and Statistics, *Census of the Philippines, 1948* (Manila, 1951). 1955 figures: IUR estimates.

[89]

RYUKYU ISLANDS

Units: NAHA: Mawashi-shi and Naha-shi.
Sources: 1950 figures: U.S. Civil Administration of the Ryukyu Islands, *Civil Affairs Activities in the Ryukyu Islands,* Vol. IV, no. I (Naha, Sept., 1956). 1956 figures: *ibid.*

SAUDI ARABIA

Sources: 1952 figures and 1954 figures: unofficial estimates in *Encyclopaedia Britannica World Atlas* (1957). Differences between estimates in this case should not be interpreted as representing growth over the two-year period.

SINGAPORE

Units: SINGAPORE: Singapore municipality and the remainder of Singapore Island.
Sources: 1947 figures: M.V. del Tufo, *Malaya: A Report on the 1947 Census of Population* (London: Crown Agents for the Colonies, n.d.). 1955 figures: estimates provided by Singapore officials.

SYRIA

Sources: 1953 figures: *Encyclopaedia Britannica World Atlas* (1957). 1955 figures: official estimates supplied by the Department of Statistics, Ministry of National Economy, Republic of Syria. (Differences between figures may be due partly to differences in coverage.)

THAILAND

Units: BANGKOK (KRUNG THEP): changwats of Phra-nakhorn (including Bangkok municipality) and Thonburi.
Sources: 1947 figures: Thailand, Central Statistical Office, *Statistical Year Book, 1952* (Bangkok, 1953). 1955 figures: IUR estimates.

TURKEY

Units: ADANA: Adana city. ANKARA: districts of Ankara and Çankaya. BURSA: Bursa city. ESKİŞEHİR: Eskişehir city. İSTANBUL: districts of Adalar, Bakirköy, Beşiktaş, Beykoz, Beyoğlu, Eminönü, Eyüp, Fatih, Kadıköy, Sarıyer, and Üsküdar. İZMİR: İzmir district.

Sources: 1950 figures: final figures for 1950 population census as quoted in Turkey, Prime Ministry, Central Statistical Office, *1955 Population Census of Turkey* (Ankara, 1957). 1955 figures: provisional results of 1955 population census, *ibid.*

VIETNAM, NORTH

Sources: 1951 figures: official estimates reported in Vietnam, Institut de la Statistique et des Études Économiques du Viêt-Nam, *Annuaire Statistique du Viêt-Nam,* Vol. I, 1949–50 (1951). 1955 figures: IUR estimates.

VIETNAM, SOUTH

Sources: 1951 figures: Vietnam, Institut de la Statistique et des Études Économiques du Viêt-Nam, *Annuaire Statistique du Viêt-Nam,* Vol. I, 1949–50 (1951) and Vol. II, 1950–51 (1952). 1955 figures: IUR estimates.

Section VI: EUROPE

AUSTRIA

Units: GRAZ: Graz city. INNSBRUCK: city of Innsbruck and political district of Innsbruck Land. LINZ: city of Linz and political district of Linz Land. SALZBURG: Salzburg city. VIENNA (WIEN): city of Wien and political district of Baden.

Sources: 1951 figures: Austria, Österreichisches Statistisches Zentralamt, *Ergebnisse der Volkszählung vom 1. Juni 1951* (by province), (Wien, 1952). 1955 figures: for cities, Wien, Magistrat der Stadt Wien, *Statistisches Jahrbuch der Stadt Wien für das Jahr 1954* (Wien, 1955) and Magistrat der Stadt Wien, *Statistisches Jahrbuch der Stadt Wien für das Jahr 1955* (Wien, 1956); Graz, Magistrat Graz, Statistisches Amt, *Statistisches Jahrbuch der Landeshauptstadt Graz 1955* (Graz, 1956); Innsbruck, Statistisches Amt der Stadt Innsbruck, *Statistisches Jahrbuch der Stadt Innsbruck 1954–1955* (Innsbruck, 1956); Linz, Statistisches Amt, *Statistisches Jahrbuch der Stadt Linz 1955* (Linz, 1956); Salzburg, Magistrat Salzburg, Statistik, *Statistisches Jahrbuch der Landeshauptstadt Salzburg 1955* (Salzburg, 1956); for Innsbruck, Linz, and Vienna M.A.'s, IUR estimates.

[91]

BELGIUM

Units: ANTWERP (ANTWERPEN): administrative arrondissement of Antwerpen. BRUSSELS (BRUXELLES): administrative arrondissement of Bruxelles. CHARLEROI: administrative arrondissement of Charleroi. GHENT (GENT): administrative arrondissement of Gent. LIÈGE: administrative arrondissement of Liège.

Sources: 1947 figures: census reports of December 31, 1947 as communicated to IUR by Professor M. R. Olbrechts, Institut de Sociologie Solvay, Université Libre de Bruxelles. 1956 figures: official estimates from Belgium, Institut National de Statistique, *Annuaire Statistique de la Belgique et du Congo Belge, 1956* (Bruxelles, 1956).

BULGARIA

Units: SOFIA (SOFIYA): Sofiya city proper and the surrounding communities under jurisdiction of the city government.

Sources: 1946 figures and 1956 figures: "Za broya na naseleniyeto na Narodna Republika Bulgariya . . . 1.XII.1956 godina" (extract from *Rabotnicheskoye Delo,* Jan. 1, 1957, made available to IUR through the courtesy of Encyclopaedia Britannica). 1946 figure for Sofiya (1946 limits): Statistical Office of the United Nations, Department of Economic and Social Affairs, *Demographic Yearbook, 1955* (New York, 1955).

CZECHOSLOVAKIA

Sources: 1950 figures: Czechoslovakia, Státní Úřad Statistický, *Statistická Ročenka Republiky Československé 1957* (Praha, 1957). 1955 figures: estimates provided by the State Statistical Office of Czechoslovakia.

DENMARK

Units: AALBORG: cities of Aalborg and Nørre Sundby; communes of Hasseris and Sundby-Hvorup. AARHUS: city of Aarhus; communes of Aaby, Brabrand-Sønder Aarslev, Hasle-Skejby-Lisbjerg, Holme-Tranbjerg, Vejlby-Riisskov, and Viby. COPENHAGEN (KØBENHAVN): city of København; communes of Ballerup-Maaløv, Birkerød, Brøndbyerne,

Dragør, Farum, Frederiksberg, Gentofte, Gladsaxe, Glostrup, Greve-Kildebrønde, Herlev, Herstederne, Høje-Taastrup, Hørsholm, Hvidovre, Lyngby-Taarbaek, Rødovre, Søllerød, Store Magleby, Taarnby, Vaerløse, and Vallensbaek. ODENSE: city of Odense; communes of Allese-Naesbyhoved Broby, Dalum, Paarup, and Sanderum.

Sources: 1950 figures and 1955 figures: Denmark, Statistiske Departement, *Folkemaengden 1. Oktober 1955 og Danmarks Administrative Inddeling* (København, 1957).

FINLAND

Units: HELSINKI: city of Helsinki; towns of Grankulla (Kauniainen), Järvenpää, and Kerava; communes of Espoo, Helsingin mlk., and Tuusula. TAMPERE: city of Tampere; town of Nokia; communes of Lempäälä and Pirkkala. TURKU: city of Turku; communes of Kaarina and Raisio.

Sources: 1950 figures: Tilastollinen Päätoimisto, *Vuoden 1950 Yleinen Väestölaskenta (1950 Population Census),* Suomen Virallinen Tilasto, VI Väestötilastoa C 102 (Helsinki, 1956). 1955 figures: official estimates provided by the Central Statistical Office of Finland, Helsinki.

FRANCE

Units: ANGERS: 3 cantons of Angers. BORDEAUX: 7 cantons of Bordeaux; cantons of Carbon-Blanc and Pessac. BREST: 3 cantons of Brest; canton of Landerneau. CLERMONT-FERRAND: 4 cantons of Clermont-Ferrand and 2 cantons of Riom. DIJON: 4 cantons of Dijon. DOUAI: 3 cantons of Douai. GRENOBLE: 3 cantons of Grenoble; canton of Sassenage. LE HÂVRE: 6 cantons of Le Hâvre; canton of Montivilliers. LE MANS: 3 cantons of Le Mans. LENS—HÉNIN-LIÉTARD: cantons of Carvin, Lens, Liévin, and Vimy. LILLE: 8 cantons of Lille, 3 cantons of Roubaix, and 3 cantons of Tourcoing; cantons of Armentières, Cysoing, Haubourdin, Lannoy, Pont-à-Marcq, Quesnoy-sur-Deûle, and Seclin. LIMOGES: communes of Isle, Le Palais-sur-Vienne, Limoges, and Panazol. LYON: in Isère department, cantons of Meyzieux and St-Symphorien-d'Ozon; in Rhône department, 12 cantons of Lyon, and cantons of Givors, Limonest, Neuville-sur-Saône, St-Genis-Laval, Vaugneray, and Villeurbanne. MARSEILLE: 12 cantons of Marseille; cantons of Aubagne, Gardanne, La Ciotat, Martigues, and Roquevaire. METZ: commune of Metz; canton of Metz-Campagne. MONTPELLIER: communes of Castelnau-le-Lez and Montpellier. MULHOUSE: 2 cantons of Mulhouse; cantons of Altkirch, Cernay, and Habsheim. NANCY: 4 cantons of Nancy; cantons of Pont-à-Mousson and St-Nicolas-de-Port. NANTES: 7 cantons of Nantes; canton of Bouaye. NICE: 4 cantons of Nice; cantons of Beausoleil, Menton, and Villefranche. ORLÉANS: 5 cantons of Orléans. PARIS: Seine department; in Seine-et-Marne department, cantons of Brie-Comte-Robert, Claye-Souilly, Lagny, and Tournan-en-Brie; in Seine-et-Oise department, 3 cantons of Versailles, and cantons of Argenteuil, Arpajon, Aulnay-sous-Bois, Boissy-St-Léger, Chevreuse, Corbeil-Essonnes, Écouen, Gonesse, Le Raincy, L'Isle-Adam, Longjumeau, Maisons-Laffitte, Marly-le-Roi, Montmorency, Palaiseau, Poissy, Pontoise, St-Germain-en-Laye, Sèvres, Taverny, and Villeneuve-St-Georges. REIMS: 4 cantons of Reims. RENNES: 4 cantons of Rennes. ROUEN: 6 cantons of Rouen; cantons of Boos, Darnétal, Elbeuf, Grand-Couronne, Maromme, and Sotteville-lès-Rouen. SAINT-ÉTIENNE: 4 cantons of St-Étienne; cantons of Firminy, Le Chambon-Feugerolles, Rive-de-Gier, St-Chamond, and St-Héand. STRASBOURG: commune of Strasbourg; cantons of Brumath, Geispolsheim, and Schiltigheim. TOULON: 4 cantons of Toulon; cantons of Hyères, La Seyne-sur-Mer, and Ollioules. TOULOUSE: 4 cantons of Toulouse. TOURS: 3 cantons of Tours.

Sources: 1946 figures: France, Institut National de le Statistique et des Études Économiques, *Résultats Statistiques du Recensement Général de la Population effectué le 10 Mars 1946* (Paris, 1951). 1954 figures: France, Institut National de la Statistique et des Études Économiques, *Recensement de 1954, Population de la France, Départements, arrondissements, cantons et communes (Métropole)* (Paris, 1954).

GERMANY, EAST

Units: BERLIN, EAST: East Berlin (Ost-Berlin); city (Stadtkreis) of Potsdam; districts (Landkreise) of Bernau, Fürstenwalde, Königs-Wusterhausen, Nauen, Oranienburg, Potsdam,

Strausberg, and Zossen. BERLIN, EAST AND WEST: East Berlin (Ost-Berlin); West Berlin; city of Potsdam; districts of Bernau, Fürstenwalde, Königs-Wusterhausen, Nauen, Oranienburg, Potsdam, Strausberg, and Zossen. DESSAU: city of Dessau; districts of Gräfenhainichen and Rosslau. DRESDEN: city of Dresden; districts of Dresden and Freital. ERFURT: Erfurt city and district. GERA: Gera city and district. GÖRLITZ: Görlitz city and district. HALLE: city of Halle; districts of Merseburg and Saalkreis. JENA: Jena city and district. KARL-MARX-STADT (CHEMNITZ): city of Karl-Marx-Stadt; districts of Flöha and Karl-Marx-Stadt. LEIPZIG: Leipzig city and district. MAGDEBURG: city of Magdeburg; districts of Schönebeck, Wanzleben, and Wolmirstedt. ROSTOCK: Rostock city and district. ZWICKAU: city of Zwickau; districts of Werdau and Zwickau.

Sources: 1950 figures and 1955 figures: official estimates from Statistisches Zentralamt, Statistisches Jahrbuch der Deutschen Demokratischen Republik (Berlin, 1956).

GERMANY, WEST

Units: AACHEN: Aachen city (Stadtkreis) and district (Landkreis). AUGSBURG: Augsburg city and district. BERLIN, WEST: West Berlin. BERLIN, EAST AND WEST: East Berlin; West Berlin; city of Potsdam; districts of Bernau, Fürstenwalde, Königs-Wusterhausen, Nauen, Oranienburg, Potsdam, Strausberg, and Zossen. BIELEFELD: Bielefeld city and district. BONN: city of Bonn; districts of Bonn and Siegkreis. BRAUNSCHWEIG (BRUNSWICK): city of Braunschweig; districts of Braunschweig and Wolfenbüttel. BREMEN: cities of Bremen and Delmenhorst; district of Wesermarsch; commune (Gemeinde)[a] of Hasbergen. BREMERHAVEN: Bremerhaven city. COLOGNE (KÖLN): cities of Köln and Leverkusen; districts of Bergheim, Köln, and Rheinisch-Bergischer Kreis. DARMSTADT: city of Darmstadt; districts of Darmstadt and Dieburg. DÜSSELDORF: cities of Düsseldorf and Neuss; district of Grevenbroich. ESSEN—DORTMUND—DUISBURG (INNER RUHR): cities of Bochum, Bottrop, Castrop-Rauxel, Dortmund, Duisburg, Essen, Gelsenkirchen, Gladbeck,

---

[a] Hasbergen commune, in Oldenburg district, included as a connecting link between the cities of Bremen and Delmenhorst;

[95]

Hagen i. W., Herne, Iserlohn, Lünen, Mülheim a.d. Ruhr, Oberhausen, Recklinghausen, Wanne-Eickel, Wattenscheid, and Witten; districts of Dinslaken, Düsseldorf-Mettmann, Ennepe-Ruhr-Kreis, Iserlohn, Moers, and Recklinghausen. FLENSBURG: Flensburg city and district. FRANKFURT AM MAIN: cities of Frankfurt am Main, Hanau, and Offenbach; districts of Friedberg, Gross Gerau, Hanau, Main-Taunus-Kreis, Obertaunuskreis, and Offenbach. FREIBURG: Freiburg city. HAMBURG: city of Hamburg; districts of Pinneberg and Stormarn. HAMM: city of Hamm; communes (Gemeinde)[b] of Berge, Bockum-Hövel, Braam-Ostwennemar, Heessen, Herringen, Pelkum, Werries, Westtünnen, and Wiescherhofen. HANNOVER: city of Hannover; districts of Burgdorf, Hannover, and Neustadt. HILDESHEIM: city of Hildesheim; district of Hildesheim-Marienburg. KARLSRUHE: city of Karlsruhe; districts of Bruchsal and Karlsruhe. KASSEL: city of Kassel; districts of Kassel, Melsungen, and Münden. KIEL: Kiel city. KOBLENZ: Koblenz city and district. KREFELD—MÖNCHEN GLADBACH—RHEYDT: cities of Krefeld, Mönchen-Gladbach, Rheydt, and Viersen; district of Kempen-Krefeld. LÜBECK: city of Lübeck; district of Eutin. MANNHEIM—LUDWIGSHAFEN—HEIDELBERG: cities of Frankenthal, Heidelberg, Ludwigshafen, Mannheim, Speyer, and Worms; districts of Bergstrasse, Frankenthal, Heidelberg, Ludwigshafen, Mannheim, and Speyer. MUNICH (MÜNCHEN): city of München; districts of Dachau, Fürstenfeldbruck, München, and Starnberg. MÜNSTER: Münster city and district. NUREMBERG (NÜRNBERG): cities of Fürth, Nürnberg, and Schwabach; districts of Fürth, Lauf, and Schwabach. OLDENBURG: Oldenburg i. O. city. OSNABRÜCK: Osnabrück city and district. PFORZHEIM: Pforzheim city and district. REGENSBURG: Regensburg city. SAARBRÜCKEN: Saarbrücken city and district. SALZGITTER: Salzgitter city. STUTTGART: city of Stuttgart; districts of Böblingen, Esslingen, Leonberg, Ludwigsburg, and Waiblingen. WIESBADEN—MAINZ: cities of Mainz and Wies-

---

[b] M.A. defined in terms of communes because none of the three districts adjoining the city exhibits sufficient integration to justify its inclusion though all three include communes whose integration with the city is evident.

[96]

baden; district of Rheingaukreis. WILHELMSHAVEN: Wilhelmshaven city. WUPPERTAL—SOLINGEN—REMSCHEID: cities of Remscheid, Solingen, and Wuppertal; district of Rhein-Wupper-Kreis.

Sources: 1950 figures: Statistisches Bundesamt, *Statistisches Jahrbuch für die Deutschen Bundesländer 1952* (Wiesbaden, 1952); Statistisches Bundesamt, *Statistische Berichte: Die Wohnbevölkerung in den Kreisfreien Städten und Landkreisen des Bundesgebietes am 31.12.1955* (Wiesbaden, 1956); Baden-Württemberg, Statistisches Landesamt, *Gemeinde- und Kreisstatistik Baden-Württemberg 1950*, Teil I–III, Statistik von Baden-Württemberg, Band 3 (Stuttgart, 1952–53); Bayern, Statistisches Landesamt, *Bayerische Gemeinde- und Kreisstatistik 1949/1950*, Beiträge zur Statistik Bayerns, Heft 177, Band 1, 3, 4, 5 (München, 1952); Bremen, Statistisches Landesamt, *Gemeinde-Statistik,* Folge I (Bremen, 1952); Hessen, Statistisches Landesamt, *Hessische Gemeindestatistik 1950,* Heft 1–2, Beiträge zur Statistik Hessens Nr. 48 (Wiesbaden, 1952); Niedersachsen, Amt für Landesplanung und Statistik, *Gemeindestatistik für Niedersachsen ... 1950,* Teil I–II (Hannover, 1952–53); Nordrhein-Westfalen, Statistisches Landesamt, *Gemeindestatistik des Landes Nordrhein-Westfalen ... 1950,* Beiträge zur Statistik des Landes Nordrhein-Westfalen, Heft 15 (Düsseldorf, 1952); Rheinland-Pfalz, Statistisches Landesamt, *Gemeindestatistik von Rheinland-Pfalz ... 1950,* Statistik von Rheinland-Pfalz, Band 21 (Bad Ems, 1952). 1955 figures: Statistisches Bundesamt, *Statistisches Jahrbuch für die Deutschen Bundesländer 1956* (Wiesbaden, 1956); Statistisches Bundesamt, *Statistische Berichte: Die Wohnbevölkerung in den Kreisfreien Städten und Landkreisen des Bundesgebietes am 31. 12. 1955* (Wiesbaden, 1956); for Saarland, Statistisches Bundesamt, *Statistische Berichte: Wohnbevölkerung und Vertriebene in den Kreisfreien Städten und Landkreisen des Bundesgebietes am 25. 9. 1956* (Wiesbaden, 1957).

GREECE

Units: ATHENS (ATHÍNAI): identical with Greater Athens as presented in official Greek statistics; corresponds to the former Administration of the Capital District. SALONIKA (THESSALONÍKA): identical with Greater Salonika as presented in official Greek statistics; comprises the municipality of Salonika and the municipalities and commune which were originally a part of it but have since become detached.

Sources: 1951 figures: Greece, National Statistical Service, *Statistical Yearbook of Greece, 1956* (Athens, 1957). 1955 figures: IUR estimates.

HUNGARY

Sources: 1949 figures and 1954 figures: Hungary, Központi Statisztikai Hivatal, *Statisztikai Évkönyv 1949–1955* (Budapest, c. 1957); 1954 figures rounded to nearest hundred by IUR.

IRELAND (EIRE)

Units: (Note: standard abbreviations have been used for County Borough, Urban District, and Rural District.) CORK (CORCAIGH): Cork CB, Cobh UD, and Cork RD. DUBLIN (BAILE ATHA CLIATH): Dublin CB, Dún Laoghaire borough, Celbridge No. 2 RD, Dublin North RD, Dublin South RD, and Rathdown No. 1 RD.

Sources: 1951 figures and 1956 figures: Ireland, Central Statistics Office, *Census of Population of Ireland, 1956* (Dublin, 1957).

ITALY

Units: BARI: communes of Bari and Valenzano. BÈRGAMO: communes of Almè, Almenno San Bartolomeo, Almenno San Salvatore, Alzano Lombardo, Ambìvere, Azzano San Pàolo, Bèrgamo, Brembate di Sopra, Curno, Dàlmine, Gorle, Grassòbbio, Làllio, Levate, Mapello, Mozzo, Nembro, Òrio al Sèrio, Òsio Sopra, Òsio Sotto, Paladina, Pedrengo, Ponterànica, Ponte San Pietro, Pradalunga, Presezzo, Rànica, Selvino, Seriate, Sorìsole, Stezzano, Torre Boldone, Treviolo, Valbrembo, Verdellino, Verdello, Villa d'Almè, and Villa di Sèrio. BOLOGNA: communes of Bologna and

Casalècchio di Reno. BRÈSCIA: communes of Bovezzo, Brèscia, Castel Mella, Cellàtica, Nave (including new commune of Caino), Roncadelle, and San Zeno Navìglio. BUSTO ARSÌZIO—LEGNANO—GALLARATE: in Milano province, communes of Arconate, Buscate, Busto Garolfo, Canegrate, Cerro Maggiore, Legnano, Magnago, Nerviano, Parabiago, Rescaldina, San Giòrgio su Legnano, and San Vittore Olona; in Varese province, communes of Busto Arsìzio, Cardano al Campo, Cassano Magnago, Castellanza, Fagnano Olona, Ferno, Gallarate, Gorla Maggiore, Gorla Minore, Lonate Pozzolo, Marnate, Olgiate Olona, Samarate, and Solbiate Olona. CÀGLIARI: communes of Càgliari, Quartu Sant'Èlena, and Selàrgius. CARRARA—MASSA: communes of Carrara, Massa, and Montignoso. CATÀNIA: communes of Catània, Gravina di Catània, and Sant'Àgata li Battiati. COMO: communes of Albese con Cassano, Blèvio, Brunate, Capiago Intimiano, Carate Ùrio, Casnate con Bernate, Cernòbbio, Como, Girònico, Grandate, Lieto Colle (including new communes of Cavallasca, Drezzo, and Parè), Lipomo, Masliànico, Moltràsio, Montano Lucino, Montòrfano, San Fermo della Battàglia, Senna Comasco, Tavernèrio, and Torno. FLORENCE (FIRENZE): communes of Campi Bisènzio, Fièsole, Firenze, Lastra a Signa, Scandicci, Sesto Fiorentino, and Signa. GENOA (GÈNOVA): communes of Arenzano, Bogliasco, Campomorone, Cerànesi, Gènova, Mele, Mignànego, Pieve Lìgure, Sant'Olcese, and Serra Riccò. LA SPÈZIA: communes of Àrcola, Follo, La Spèzia, Lèrici, Portovènere, Riccò del Golfo di Spèzia, Riomaggiore, Santo Stèfano di Magra, Sarzana, and Vezzano Lìgure. LEGHORN (LIVORNO): Livorno commune. MESSINA: Messina commune. MILAN (MILANO): in Como province, communes of Cabiate, Cernusco Montevecchia, Lomagna, and Osnago; in Milano province, communes of Agrate Brianza, Aicùrzio, Albiate, Àrcore, Arese, Arluno, Assago, Barèggio, Barlassina, Bellinzago Lombardo, Bellusco, Bernarèggio, Biassono, Bollate, Bovìsio-Masciago, Bresso, Brughèrio, Buccinasco, Burago di Mòlgora, Busnago, Bùssero, Cambiago, Camparada, Caponago, Carnate, Carugate, Cassina de' Pecchi, Cavenago di Brianza, Ceriano Laghetto, Cernusco sul Navìglio, Cesano Boscone, Cesano Maderno,

Cesate, Cinisello Bàlsamo, Cogliate, Cologno Monzese, Concorezzo, Cormano, Cornaredo, Cornate d'Adda, Correzzana, Còrsico, Cusano Milanino, Dèsio, Gaggiano, Garbagnate Milanese, Gessate, Gorgonzola, Inzago, Lainate, Lazzate, Lentate sul Sèveso, Lesmo, Limbiate, Lissone, Locate di Triulzi, Machèrio, Meda, Melzo, Mezzago, Milano, Misinto, Monza, Muggiò, Nova Milanese, Novate Milanese, Òpera, Ornago, Ossona, Paderno Dugnano, Pero, Pessano con Bornago, Pioltello, Pogliano Milanese, Pozzuolo Martesana, Pregnana Milanese, Rho, Roncello, Ronco Briantino, Rossano, San Donato Milanese, San Giuliano Milanese, Santo Stèfano Ticino, Sedriano, Segrate, Senago, Seregno, Sesto San Giovanni, Sèttimo Milanese, Sèveso, Solaro, Sovico, Sulbiate, Trezzano sul Navìglio, Triùggio, Usmate Velate, Vanzago, Varedo, Vedano al Lambro, Vignate, Villasanta, Vimercate, Vimodrone, and Vittuone. MÒDENA: Mòdena commune. NAPLES (NÀPOLI): in Caserta province, commune of Sant'Arpino; in Nàpoli province, communes of Afragola, Arzano, Calvizzano, Cardito, Casalnuovo di Nàpoli, Casandrino, Casavatore, Casòria, Cèrcola, Crispano, Frattamaggiore, Frattaminore, Grumo Nevano, Melito di Nàpoli, Mugnano di Nàpoli, Nàpoli, Pomigliano d'Arco, Pòrtici, Pozzuoli, Resina, San Giòrgio a Cremano, San Sebastiano al Vesùvio (including new commune of Volla), Sant'Àntimo, and Torre del Greco. PADUA (PÀDOVA): communes of Cadòneghe, Noventa Padovana, and Pàdova. PALERMO: Palermo commune. PARMA: Parma commune. RÈGGIO DI CALÀBRIA: Règgio di Calàbria commune. ROME (ROMA): communes of Albano Laziale, Castel Gandolfo, Frascati, Grottaferrata, Guidònia Montecèlio, Marino, Monterotondo, Roma, and Tìvoli. SALERNO: communes of Baronissi, Cava de' Tirreni, Pellezzano, Salerno, and Vietri sul Mare. TÀRANTO: Tàranto commune. TRIESTE: communes of Monrupino, Mùggia, San Dorligo della Valle, and Trieste. TURIN (TORINO): communes of Alpignano, Beinasco, Bòrgaro Torinese, Brandizzo, Buttigliera Alta, Candiolo, Caselette, Caselle Torinese, Collegno, Druento, Grugliasco, Moncalieri, Nichelino, Orbassano, Pecetto Torinese, Pianezza, Rìvoli, Rosta, San Francesco al Campo, San Maurìzio Canavese, San Màuro Torinese, Sèttimo Torinese,

Torino, Trofarello, Venaria, and Vinovo. VENICE (VEN-
ÈZIA): communes of Mira, Spinea, and Venèzia. VERONA:
communes of San Giovanni Lupatoto and Verona.
Sources: 1951 figures: Italy, Istituto Centrale di Statistica, *IX
Censimento Generale della Popolazione 1951,* Vol. I, "Dati
Sommari per Comune" (a separate part for each province)
(Roma, 1954–1956). 1955 figures: Italy, Istituto Centrale
di Statistica, *Popolazione e Circoscrizioni Amministrative
dei Comune . . . 1954, 1955, 1956* (Roma, 1957). 1951 figures
and 1955 figures for Vatican City: Statistical Office of the
United Nations, Department of Economic and Social Af-
fairs, *Demographic Yearbook, 1956* (New York, 1956).

MALTA AND GOZO

Units: VALLETTA: localities of Attard, Balzan, Birkirkara,
Cospicua, Floriana, Gzira, Hamrun, Kalkara, Lija, Luqa,
Marascala, Marsa, Msida, Paola, Pieta, Qormi, St. Julians,
Santa Vennera, Senglea, Sliema, Tarxien, Valletta, Vittor-
iosa, and Zabbar.
Sources: 1948 figures: Malta, Office of Statistics, *Eleventh
Census of the Maltese Islands June 14, 1948* (Valletta, 1949).
1955 figures: estimates by the Office of Statistics, Malta.

NETHERLANDS

Units: AMSTERDAM: communes of Amsterdam, Assendelft,
Diemen, Koog a/d Zaan, Krommenie, Landsmeer, Muiden,
Nieuwer-Amstel, Oostzaan, Ouder-Amstel, Uitgeest, West-
zaan, Wormer, Wormerveer, Zaandam, and Zaandijk. ARN-
HEM: communes of Arnhem, Renkum, Rheden, Rozendaal,
and Westervoort. DORDRECHT: communes of Dordrecht,
's-Gravendeel, Papendrecht, Sliedrecht, and Zwijndrecht.
EINDHOVEN: communes of Eindhoven, Geldrop, Heeze,
Valkenswaard, Veldhoven, and Waalre. ENSCHEDE—HEN-
GELO: communes of Borne, Enschede, Hengelo, and Stad-
Delden. GRONINGEN: communes of Groningen, Haren, and
Hoogkerk. HAARLEM—VELSEN: communes of Bennebroek,
Beverwijk, Bloemendaal, Haarlem, Heemstede, Velsen, and
Zandvoort. HEERLEN—KERKRADE: communes of Amsten-
rade, Brunssum, Bocholtz, Eijgelshoven, Heerlen, Hoens-
broek, Kerkrade, Merkelbeek, Nieuwenhagen, Nuth, Oirs-

beek, Schaesberg, Schinnen, Schinveld, Simpelveld, Spau-
beek, Ubach over Worms, and Voerendaal. LEIDEN: communes of Koudekerk a/d Rijn, Leiden, Leiderdorp, Oegst-
geest, and Voorschoten. NIJMEGEN: communes of Groes-
beek, Nijmegen, and Ubbergen. ROTTERDAM: communes of
Alblasserdam, Barendrecht, Capelle a/d IJssel, Hendrik-
Ido-Ambacht, Krimpen a/d IJssel, Krimpen a/d Lek, Maas-
sluis, Ouderkerk a/d IJssel, Poortugaal, Ridderkerk, Rotterdam, Schiedam, Spijkenisse, and Vlaardingen. THE
HAGUE ('s-GRAVENHAGE): communes of Delft, 's-Gravenhage, Leidschendam, Rijswijk, Voorburg, and Wassenaar.
TILBURG: communes of Goirle and Tilburg. UTRECHT:
communes of Breukelen-Nijenrode, Breukelen-St. Pieters,
Bunnik, De Bilt, Doorn, Driebergen-Rijsenburg, IJsselstein,
Jutphaas, Maarssen, Maarsseveen, Maartensdijk, Utrecht,
Vianen, Vreeswijk, Zeist, and Zuilen.

Sources: 1947 figures: Netherlands, Centraal Bureau voor de
Statistiek, *12e Volkstelling,* Deel 1 ('s-Gravenhage, 1950).
1955 figures: Netherlands, Centraal Bureau voor de Statistiek, *Bevolking der Gemeenten van Nederland op 1 Jan-
uari 1955* (Utrecht, De Haan, 1955).

NORWAY

Units: BERGEN: city of Bergen; communes (herreder) of Åsane,
Askøy, Fana, Haus, Laksevåg, and Os. OSLO: city of Oslo;
communes (herreder) of Ås, Asker, Baerum, Frogn, Lille-
strøm, Lørenskog, Nesodden, Oppegård, Raelingen, Sked-
smo, and Ski.

Sources: 1950 figures: Norway, Statistisk Sentralbyrå, *Folke-
tellingen 1 Desember 1950,* Vol. I (Oslo, 1953). 1954 figures:
Municipal Office of Statistics of Oslo, *Statistisk Årbok for
Oslo, 1956* (Oslo, 1957); Municipal Office of Statistics for
Bergen, *Statistisk Årbok for Bergen, 1955* (Bergen, 1956);
and IUR estimates.

POLAND

Units: BYDGOSZCZ: Bydgoszcz city. CZĘSTOCHOWA: Częstochowa city. GDAŃSK—GDYNIA: cities of Gdańsk, Gdynia,
and Sopot. KATOWICE—ZABRZE—BYTOM (UPPER SILESIA):
cities of Będzin, Bytom, Chorzów, Czeladź, Dąbrowa Gór-

nicza, Gliwice, Katowice, Mysłowice, Nowy Bytom, Ruda, Siemianowice Śląskie, Sosnowiec, Świętochłowice, Szopienice, Tychy, and Zabrze; districts of Będzin, Gliwice, Tarnowskie Góry, and Tychy. Kraków (Cracow): Kraków city. Łódź: cities of Łódź, Pabianice, and Zgierz; district of Łódź. Lublin: Lublin city. Poznań: Poznań city. Szczecin: Szczecin city. Wałbrzych: Wałbrzych city and district. Warsaw (Warszawa): cities of Pruszków and Warszawa; districts of Nowy Dwór Mazowiecki, Otwock, Piaseczno, Pruszków, and Wołomin. Wrocław (Breslau): Wrocław city.

Sources: 1950 figures: Poland, Główny Urząd Statystyczny, *Rocznik Statystyczny 1957* (Warszawa, 1957); and material supplied to IUR from Polish government sources. 1950 figures for four M.A.'s are partly estimated by IUR. 1956 figures: Poland, Główny Urząd Statystyczny, *Rocznik Statystyczny 1957* (Warszawa, 1957).

PORTUGAL

Units: Lisbon (Lisboa): concelhos of Almada, Barreiro, Cascais, Lisboa, Loures, Moita, Oeiras, and Seixal. Oporto (Pôrto): concelhos of Gondomar, Maia, Matosinhos, Pôrto, and Vila Nova de Gaia.

Sources: 1950 figures: Portugal, Instituto Nacional de Estatística, *IX Recenseamento Geral—1950,* Vols. I, II, and III (Lisboa, 1952–). 1955 figures: IUR estimates.

ROMANIA

Source: 1948 figures and 1956 figures: Romania, Direcţiunea Centrală de Statistică, *Anuarul Statistic al R.P.R.* (Bucureşti, 1957).

SPAIN

Units: Alicante: Alicante municipio. Barcelona: municipios of Badalona, Barcelona, Cornellá, Esplugas, Hospitalet, Molíns de Rey, Moncada y Reixach, Mongat, Prat del Llobregat, Ripollet, San Adrián de Besós, San Baudilio de Llobregat, San Cugat del Vallés, San Felíu de Llobregat, San Juan Despí, San Justo Desvern, Santa Coloma de Cervelló, Santa Coloma de Gramanet, San Vicente dels Horts, and Sardanyola. BILBAO: municipios of Arrigorriaga, Baracaldo, Basauri, Bilbao, Echévarri, Galdácano, Guecho, Lejona, Lujua, Portugalete, San Salvador del Valle, Santurce-Antiguo, Santurce-Ortuella, and Sestao. CÁDIZ: Cádiz municipio. CÓRDOBA: Córdoba municipio. GIJÓN: Gijón municipio. GRANADA: municipios of Armilla, Granada, and Maracena. LA CORUÑA: La Coruña municipio. LAS PALMAS DE GRAN CANARIA: Las Palmas municipio. MADRID: municipios of Getafe, Leganés, Madrid, and Villaverde. MÁLAGA: Málaga municipio. MURCIA: Murcia municipio. OVIEDO: Oviedo municipio. PALMA DE MALLORCA: Palma de Mallorca municipio. SAN SEBASTIÁN: municipios of Hernani, Lezo, Pasajes, Rentería, and San Sebastián. SANTA CRUZ DE TENERIFE: Santa Cruz de Tenerife municipio. SANTANDER: Santander municipio. SEVILLE (SEVILLA): municipios of Camas, San Juan de Aznalfarache, and Sevilla. VALENCIA: municipios of Alboraya, Aldaya, Benetúser, Burjasot, Chirivella, Cuart de Poblet, Godella, Manises, Mislata, Paiporta, Paterna, Picaña, Tabernes Blanques, Torrente, and Valencia. VALLADOLID: Valladolid municipio. VIGO: Vigo municipio. ZARAGOZA: Zaragoza municipio.

Sources: 1950 figures: Spain, Instituto Nacional de Estadística, *Censo de Población de España y territorios ... según el empadronamiento realizado el 31 de diciembre de 1950*, Vols. I and II (Madrid, 1952, 1954). 1955 figures: IUR estimates.

SWEDEN

Units: GÖTEBORG: cities of Göteborg, Kungälv, and Mölndal; communes of Angered, Askim, Kållered, Lerum, Nödinge, Partille, Råda, Säve, Starrkärr (Starrkärr section only), Tuve, and Ytterby. MALMÖ: city of Malmö; town of Lomma; commune of Burlöv. STOCKHOLM: cities of Djursholm, Lidingö, Nacka, Solna, Stockholm, Sundbyberg, and Vaxholm; towns of Danderyd, Saltsjöbaden, Sollentuna, Stocksund, and Täby; communes of Boo, Botkyrka, Huddinge, Järfälla, and Upplands-Väsby.

Sources: 1950 figures: Sweden, Statistiska Centralbyrån, *Folkräkningen den 31 December 1950*, Vol. I, Sveriges

Officiella Statistik (Stockholm, 1954). 1955 figures: Sweden, Statistiska Centralbyrån, *Statistisk Årsbok för Sverige 1956* (Stockholm, 1956).

SWITZERLAND

Units: BASEL (BÂLE): in Aargau canton, communes of Kaiseraugst, Magden, Möhlin, Mumpf, Münchwilen, Obermumpf, Rheinfelden, Stein, Wallbach, and Zeiningen; Basel-Stadt canton (entire); in Basel-Land canton, district of Arlesheim, and communes of Augst, Bubendorf, Frenkendorf, Füllinsdorf, Itingen, Lausen, Liestal, Lupsingen, Pratteln, Ramlinsburg, Seltisberg, and Ziefen; in Bern canton, communes of Burg im Leimental, Düggingen, and Grellingen; in Solothurn canton, communes of Bättwil, Büren, Dornach, Hofstetten, Metzerlen, Nuglar-Sankt Pantaleon, and Witterswil. BERN (BERNE): in Bern canton, communes of Bäriswil, Belp, Bern, Bolligen, Bremgarten bei Bern, Hindelbank, Kehrsatz, Köniz, Mattstetten, Moosseedorf, Münchenbuchsee, Muri bei Bern, Stettlen, Toffen, Urtenen, and Zollikofen. GENEVA (GENÈVE): in Genève canton, Anières, Bellevue, Bernex, Carouge, Chêne-Bougeries, Chêne-Bourg, Choulex, Collonge-Bellerive, Cologny, Confignon, Corsier, Genève, Genthod, Hermance, Lancy, Le Grand-Saconnex, Meyrin, Onex, Plan-les-Ouates, Pregny, Thônex, Troinex, Vandoeuvres, Vernier, Versoix, and Veyrier; in Vaud canton, communes of Coppet, Mies, and Tannay. LAUSANNE: in Vaud canton, communes of Belmont sur Lausanne, Bussigny sur Morges, Chavannes près Renens, Crissier, Denges, Ecublens, Epalinges, Jouxtens-Mézery, Lausanne, Lutry, Paudex, Prilly, Pully, Renens, and St-Sulpice. ZÜRICH: in Aargau canton, communes of Berikon, Killwangen, Rudolfstetten, Spreitenbach, and Widen; in Zürich canton, communes of Adliswil, Affoltern am Albis, Bassersdorf, Birmensdorf, Bonstetten, Dietikon, Dietlikon, Dübendorf, Erlenbach, Fällanden, Geroldswil, Hedingen, Herrliberg, Horgen, Kilchberg, Kloten, Küsnacht, Langnau am Albis, Männedorf, Meilen, Niederglatt, Oberengstringen, Oberglatt, Oberrieden, Obfelden, Oetwil an der Limmat, Ottenbach, Opfikon, Regensdorf, Rümlang, Rüschlikon, Schlieren, Schwerzenbach, Stäfa, Thalwil, Uetikon, Uitikon, Unterengstringen, Urdorf, Wallisellen, Wangen, Weiningen, Wettswil, Zollikon, Zumikon, and Zürich.

Sources: 1950 figures: for cities, Switzerland, Eidgenössisches Statistisches Amt, *Statistisches Jahrbuch der Schweiz, 1955* (Bern, 1956); for M.A.'s, Switzerland, Eidgenössisches Statistisches Amt, *Eidgenössische Volkszählung 1 Dezember 1950* (by canton) (Bern, 1953–1955). 1955 figures: for cities, Switzerland, Eidgenössisches Statistisches Amt, *Statistisches Jahrbuch der Schweiz, 1955* (Bern, 1956); for M.A.'s, IUR estimates.

UNITED KINGDOM: ENGLAND AND WALES

Units: (Note: The "conurbations" mentioned below are those presented in the 1951 census publications. The other local government areas included are listed by county, using standard abbreviations for County Borough, Municipal Borough, Urban District, and Rural District.) ALDERSHOT—FARNBOROUGH: in Southampton, Aldershot MB, Farnborough UD, Fleet UD, and Hartley Wintney RD; in Surrey, Farnham UD and Frimley & Camberley UD. BARNSLEY: in Yorkshire (West Riding), Barnsley CB, Cudworth UD, Darfield UD, Darton UD, Dodworth UD, Hoyland Nether UD, Penistone UD, Royston UD, Stocksbridge UD, Wombwell UD, Worsborough UD, and Penistone RD. BIRMINGHAM: West Midlands Conurbation; in Staffordshire, Brownhills UD, Cannock UD, Lichfield MB, Tamworth MB, Cannock RD, Lichfield RD, and Seisdon RD; in Warwickshire, Meriden RD and Tamworth RD; in Worcestershire, Bromsgrove UD and Bromsgrove RD. BLACKBURN—ACCRINGTON: in Lancashire, Blackburn CB, Accrington MB, Church UD, Clayton le Moors UD, Darwen MB, Great Harwood UD, Oswaldtwistle UD, Rishton UD, and Blackburn RD. BLACKPOOL: in Lancashire, Blackpool CB, Fleetwood MB, Lytham St. Anne's MB, Poulton le Fylde UD, Preesall UD, and Thornton Cleveleys UD. BOURNEMOUTH—POOLE: in Dorset, Poole MB and Wimborne Minster UD; in Southampton, Bournemouth CB and Christchurch MB. BRIGHTON—WORTHING: in Sussex (East), Brighton CB, Hove MB, and Portslade-by-Sea UD; in Sussex (West), Shoreham-by-Sea UD, Southwick UD,

Worthing MB, and Worthing RD. BRISTOL: in Gloucester-
shire, Bristol CB, Kingswood UD, Mangotsfield UD, Sod-
bury RD, Thornbury RD, and Warmley RD; in Somerset,
Clevedon UD, Keynsham UD, Portishead UD, and Long
Ashton RD. BURNLEY—NELSON: in Lancashire, Burnley
CB, Barrowford UD, Brierfield UD, Colne MB, Nelson
MB, Padiham UD, Trawden UD, and Burnley RD. CAM-
BRIDGE: in Cambridgeshire, Cambridge MB and Chesterton
RD. CARDIFF—RHONDDA: in Glamorganshire, Cardiff CB,
Barry MB, Caerphilly UD, Mountain Ash UD, Penarth
UD, Pontypridd UD, Rhondda UD, Cardiff RD. and
Llantrisant & Llantwitfardre RD; in Monmouthshire,
Bedwas & Machen UD. CHATHAM—ROCHESTER—GIL-
LINGHAM: in Kent, Chatham MB, Gillingham MB,
Rochester MB, and Strood RD. CHESTERFIELD: in Derby-
shire, Bolsover UD, Chesterfield MB, Clay Cross UD,
Staveley UD, Chesterfield RD, and Clowne RD. COVENTRY:
in Leicestershire, Hinckley UD; in Warwickshire, Coventry
CB, Bedworth UD, Kenilworth UD, Nuneaton MB, Royal
Leamington Spa MB, Warwick MB, Atherstone RD, Rugby
RD, Southam RD, and Warwick RD. DARLINGTON—AUCK-
LAND: in Durham, Darlington CB, Bishop Auckland UD,
Shildon UD, and Darlington RD. DERBY: in Derbyshire,
Derby CB, Alfreton UD, Belper UD, Heanor UD, Ripley
UD, Belper RD, Repton RD, and Shardlow RD. DON-
CASTER: in Yorkshire (West Riding), Doncaster CB, Ad-
wick le Street UD, Bentley with Arksey UD, and Doncaster
RD. EXETER: in Devonshire, Exeter CB, Dawlish UD,
Exmouth UD, and St. Thomas RD. GLOUCESTER: in
Gloucestershire, Gloucester CB and Gloucester RD.
GRIMSBY: in Lincolnshire (Parts of Lindsey), Grimsby CB,
Cleethorpes MB, and Grimsby RD. HULL (KINGSTON UPON
HULL): in Yorkshire (East Riding), Kingston upon Hull
CB and Haltemprice UD. IPSWICH: in Suffolk (East),
Ipswich CB. LANCASTER—MORECAMBE: in Lancashire,
Lancaster MB, Carnforth UD, Morecambe & Heysham
MB, and Lancaster RD. LEEDS—BRADFORD: West York-
shire Conurbation; in Yorkshire (West Riding), Castleford
UD, Featherstone UD, Garforth UD, Ilkley UD, Knotting-
ley UD, Normanton UD, Otley UD, Pontefract MB, Silsden

UD, Osgoldcross RD, Tadcaster RD, Wakefield RD, and Wharfedale RD. LEICESTER: in Leicestershire, Leicester CB, Oadby UD, Wigston UD, Barrow upon Soar RD, Billesdon RD, Blaby RD, and Market Bosworth RD. LIVERPOOL: Merseyside Conurbation; in Lancashire, Southport CB, Formby UD, Ormskirk UD, Skelmersdale UD, West Lancashire RD, Whiston RD, and Prescot UD. LONDON: Greater London Conurbation; in Berkshire, Maidenhead MB, New Windsor MB, Cookham RD, Easthampstead RD, and Windsor RD; in Buckinghamshire, Beaconsfield UD, Chesham UD, Eton UD, Slough MB, Amersham RD, and Eton RD; in Essex, Southend-on-Sea CB, Basildon (Billericay) UD, Benfleet UD, Brentwood UD, Canvey Island UD, Epping UD, Harlow UD, Hornchurch UD, Rayleigh UD, Romford MB, Thurrock UD, Epping & Ongar RD, and Rochford RD; in Hertfordshire, Berkhamsted UD, Chorleywood UD, Harpenden UD, Hemel Hempstead MB, Hertford MB, Hoddesdon UD, Rickmansworth UD, St. Albans MB, Sawbridgeworth UD, Tring UD, Ware UD, Watford MB, Welwyn Garden City UD, Berkhamsted RD, Hatfield RD, Hemel Hempstead RD, Hertford RD, St. Albans RD, Ware RD, Watford RD, and Welwyn RD; in Kent, Dartford MB, Gravesend MB, Northfleet UD, Sevenoaks UD, Swanscombe UD, Dartford RD, and Sevenoaks RD; in Surrey, Caterham & Warlingham UD, Chertsey UD, Dorking UD, Egham UD, Godalming MB, Guildford MB, Leatherhead UD, Reigate MB, Walton & Weybridge UD, Woking UD, Bagshot RD, Dorking & Horley RD, Godstone RD, Guildford RD, and Hambledon RD. LUTON: in Bedfordshire, Luton MB, Dunstable MB, and Luton RD. MANCHESTER: South East Lancashire Conurbation; in Cheshire, Knutsford UD, Longdendale UD, Bucklow RD, and Tintwistle RD; in Derbyshire, Glossop MB; in Lancashire, Blackrod UD, Ramsbottom UD, and Turton UD; in Yorkshire (West Riding), Saddleworth UD. MANSFIELD—SUTTON: in Derbyshire, Blackwell RD; in Nottinghamshire, Kirkby in Ashfield UD, Mansfield MB, Mansfield Woodhouse UD, Sutton in Ashfield UD, Warsop UD, and Southwell RD. MIDDLESBROUGH—STOCKTON—WEST HARTLEPOOL: in Durham, West Hartlepool CB, Billingham UD, Hartlepool MB, Stockton on Tees MB, and Stockton RD; in Yorkshire (North Riding), Middlesbrough CB, Eston UD, Guisborough UD, Loftus UD, Redcar MB, Saltburn & Marske by the Sea UD, Skelton & Brotton UD, Thornaby on Tees MB, and Stokesley RD. NEWCASTLE UPON TYNE: Tyneside Conurbation; in Durham, Blaydon UD, Boldon UD, Chester le Street UD, Consett UD, Ryton UD, Stanley UD, Washington UD, Chester le Street RD, and Lanchester RD; in Northumberland, Prudhoe UD, Seaton Valley UD, and Castle Ward RD. NEWPORT—PONTYPOOL: in Glamorganshire, Gelligaer UD; in Monmouthshire, Newport CB, Abercarn UD, Abertillery UD, Bedwellty UD, Blaenavon UD, Caerleon UD, Cwmbran UD, Ebbw Vale UD, Mynyddislwyn UD, Nantyglo & Blaina UD, Pontypool UD, Rhymney UD, Risca UD, Tredegar UD, Usk UD, Magor & St. Mellons RD, and Pontypool RD; in Brecknockshire, Brynmawr UD. NORTHAMPTON: in Northamptonshire, Northampton CB, Brixworth RD, and Northampton RD. NORWICH: in Norfolk, Norwich CB, Blofield & Flegg RD, Forehoe & Henstead RD, and St. Faith's & Aylsham RD. NOTTINGHAM: in Derbyshire, Ilkeston UD and Long Eaton UD; in Nottinghamshire, Nottingham CB, Arnold UD, Beeston & Stapleford UD, Carlton UD, Eastwood UD, Hucknall UD, West Bridgford UD, Basford RD, and Bingham RD. OXFORD: in Berkshire, Abingdon MB and Abingdon RD; in Oxfordshire, Oxford CB, Thame UD, and Bullingdon RD. PLYMOUTH: in Cornwall, Saltash MB and Torpoint UD; in Devon, Plymouth CB and Plympton St. Mary RD. PORTSMOUTH: in Southampton, Portsmouth CB, Fareham UD, Gosport MB, and Havant & Waterloo UD. PORT TALBOT: in Glamorganshire, Bridgend UD, Glyncorwg UD, Maesteg UD, Porthcawl UD, Port Talbot MB, and Penybont RD. PRESTON: in Lancashire, Preston CB, Adlington UD, Chorley MB, Fulwood UD, Leyland UD, Longridge UD, Walton le Dale UD, Withnell UD, Chorley RD, and Preston RD. READING: in Berkshire, Reading CB, Wokingham MB, Bradfield RD, and Wokingham RD; in Oxfordshire, Henley on Thames MB and Henley RD. SAINT HELENS: in Lancashire, Saint

Helens CB, Haydock UD, and Rainford UD. SHEFFIELD: in Derbyshire, Dronfield UD; in Yorkshire (West Riding), Sheffield CB, Rotherham CB, Maltby UD, Rawmarsh UD, Kiveton Park RD, Rotherham RD, and Wortley RD. SOUTHAMPTON: in Southampton, Southampton CB, Eastleigh MB, Romsey MB, Winchester MB, New Forest RD, Romsey & Stockbridge RD, and Winchester RD. STOKE ON TRENT: in Cheshire, Alsager UD; in Staffordshire, Stoke on Trent CB, Biddulph UD, Kidsgrove UD, Leek UD, Newcastle under Lyme MB, Stone UD, Cheadle RD, Leek RD, Newcastle under Lyme RD, and Stone RD. SUNDERLAND: in Durham, Sunderland CB, Seaham UD, and Sunderland RD. SWANSEA—NEATH: in Glamorganshire, Swansea CB, Llwchwr UD, Neath MB, Gower RD, Neath RD, and Pontardawe RD. SWINDON: in Wiltshire, Swindon MB, Cricklade & Wootton Bassett RD, and Highworth RD. WARRINGTON: in Cheshire, Lymm UD and Runcorn RD; in Lancashire, Warrington CB, Newton-le-Willows UD, and Warrington RD. WIGAN—LEIGH: in Lancashire, Wigan CB, Abram UD, Ashton in Makerfield UD, Aspull UD, Atherton UD, Billinge & Winstanley UD, Golborne UD, Hindley UD, Ince in Makerfield UD, Leigh MB, Orrell UD, Standish with Langtree UD, Tyldesley UD, Upholland UD, and Wigan RD. YORK: in Yorkshire (North Riding), Flaxton RD; in Yorkshire (West Riding), York CB.

Sources: 1951 figures: England and Wales, General Register Office, *Census 1951, General Tables* (London, 1956); *Report on Usual Residence and Workplace* (London, 1956). 1956 figures: England and Wales, General Register Office, *Estimates of the Population of England and Wales, Population of Each Administrative Area at 30th June, 1956* (London, 1957).

UNITED KINGDOM: NORTHERN IRELAND

Units: BELFAST: Belfast CB; in County Antrim, Belfast RD and Lisburn RD; in County Down, Holywood UD and Castlereagh RD.

Sources: 1951 figures: Northern Ireland, Registrar-General's Division, *Census of Population of Northern Ireland, 1951, General Report* and county volumes (Belfast, 1953–1955). 1955 figures: IUR estimates.

Units: ABERDEEN: city of Aberdeen; in Aberdeenshire, district of Aberdeen; in Kincardineshire, district of Lower Deeside. DUNDEE: city of Dundee; in Angus, burgh of Monifieth and district of Monifieth; in Fifeshire, burghs of Newport-on-Tay and Tayport. EDINBURGH: city of Edinburgh; in East Lothian, burghs of Cockenzie & Port Seton, Prestonpans, and Tranent, and districts of Prestonpans and Tranent; in Midlothian, burghs of Bonnyrigg & Lasswade, Dalkeith, Loanhead, Musselburgh, and Penicuik, and districts of Currie, Lasswade, Musselburgh, Newbattle, and Penicuik; in West Lothian, burgh of Queensferry and districts of Queensferry and Uphall. GLASGOW: city of Glasgow; in Dunbartonshire, burghs of Clydebank, Kirkintilloch, and Milngavie, and districts of Cumbernauld, Kirkintilloch, New Kilpatrick, and Old Kilpatrick; in Lanarkshire, burghs of Airdrie, Coatbridge, Hamilton, Motherwell & Wishaw, and Rutherglen, and districts 4, 5, 6, 7, 8, and 9; in Renfrewshire, burghs of Barrhead, Johnstone, Paisley, and Renfrew, and districts 1, 2, 3, and 4; in Stirlingshire, district West No. 3. GREENOCK: in Renfrewshire, burghs of Gourock, Greenock, and Port Glasgow.

Sources: 1951 figures: Scotland, General Registry Office, *Report on the Fifteenth Census of Scotland,* Vol. I, parts 1–35, and Vol. IV (Edinburgh, 1952–1956). 1956 figures: official estimates reported by the Registrar-General's Office, Edinburgh.

YUGOSLAVIA

Sources: 1953 figures: Statistical Office of the United Nations, Department of Economic and Social Affairs, *Demographic Yearbook, 1955* (New York, 1955). 1955 figures: Yugoslavia, Federal Statistical Office, *Statistical Pocket Book of Yugoslavia 1957* (Belgrade, 1957).

AUSTRALIA

Units: (Note: Areas are listed as they existed at the time of the 1947 census.) ADELAIDE: municipal corporations of Adelaide, Brighton, Burnside, Campbelltown, Colonel Light Gardens, Enfield, Glenelg, Henley & Grange, Hindmarsh, Kensington & Norwood, Marion, Mitcham, Payneham, Port Adelaide, Prospect, St. Peters, Thebarton, Unley, Walkerville, West Torrens, and Woodville; district councils of Salisbury and Stirling. BRISBANE: Brisbane City community area and the remainder of Greater Brisbane municipality. MELBOURNE: cities of Box Hill, Brighton, Brunswick, Camberwell, Caulfield, Chelsea, Coburg, Collingwood, Essendon, Fitzroy, Footscray, Hawthorn, Heidelberg, Kew, Malvern, Melbourne, Moorabbin, Mordialloc, Northcote, Nunawading, Oakleigh, Port Melbourne, Prahran, Preston, Richmond, Sandringham, South Melbourne, St. Kilda, and Williamstown; borough of Ringwood; shires of Braybrook, Broadmeadows, Dandenong, Fern Tree Gully, Keilor, Mulgrave, and Werribee. NEWCASTLE: municipalities of Cessnock, Maitland, and Newcastle (Greater); shires of Kearsley and Lake Macquarie. PERTH: Perth municipality and the remainder of the Perth Metropolitan Area as reported in the 1947 census. SYDNEY: municipalities of Alexandria, Annandale, Ashfield, Auburn, Balmain, Bankstown, Bexley, Botany, Burwood, Canterbury, Concord, Darlington, Drummoyne, Dundas, Eastwood, Enfield, Ermington & Rydalmere, Erskineville, Fairfield, Glebe, Granville, Holroyd, Homebush, Hunter's Hill, Hurstville, Kogarah, Ku-ring-gai, Lane Cove, Leichhardt, Lidcombe, Manly, Marrickville, Mascot, Mosman, Newtown, North Sydney, Paddington, Parramatta, Petersham, Randwick, Redfern, Rockdale, Ryde, St. Peters, Strathfield, Sydney, Vaucluse, Waterloo, Waverley, Willoughby, and Woollahra; shires of Blacktown, Hornsby, Sutherland, and Warringah.

Sources: 1947 figures: Australia, Commonwealth Bureau of

Census and Statistics, *Census of the Commonwealth of Australia, 30th June, 1947,* "Statistician's Report" (Canberra, 1952); figure for present area of Sydney, New South Wales, Government Statistician, *Official Year Book of New South Wales, 1955,* part iii (Sydney, 1955). 1954 figures: except for Melbourne M.A. and Sydney M.A., based on the results of the 1954 census as communicated to IUR by the Commonwealth Bureau of Census and Statistics, Canberra; for Melbourne M.A. and Sydney M.A., IUR estimates.

HAWAII

Units: HONOLULU: Honolulu county, officially the "City and County of Honolulu." (The area listed as the "city" is Honolulu district, which is generally considered to represent the city proper but which has no separate municipal status.)

Sources: 1950 figures: U.S. Bureau of the Census, *United States Census of Population, 1950,* Vol. II, part 52 (Washington, 1952). 1956 figures: estimates provided through the courtesy of Rand McNally & Company. These estimates appear in the Rand McNally *Commercial Atlas and Marketing Guide, 1958.*

NEW ZEALAND

Units: (Note: counties include interior boroughs and town districts.) AUCKLAND: counties of Eden, Manukau, and Waitemata. CHRISTCHURCH: counties of Halswell, Heathcote, Paparua, and Waimairi. DUNEDIN: counties of Peninsula, Taieri, and Waikouaita. WELLINGTON: counties of Hutt and Makara.

Sources: 1951 figures and 1956 figures: New Zealand, Census and Statistics Department, *Population Census, 1956,* Vol. I (Wellington, 1957).

U.S.S.R.

Units: (Note: In the absence of most of the material necessary to delimit M.A.'s strictly comparable to those elsewhere in this study, M.A.'s have been set up for only three of the largest cities. Approximate populations for 1952 for the urban settlements and rayons in Moscow and Leningrad oblasts were compiled from lists of local election districts by Theodore Shabad and kindly made available by him to IUR. Decisions as to which units to include in each M.A. were made by IUR, primarily on the basis of the known character of the individual outlying places. IUR is indebted to Mr. Shabad for information along these lines more recent than that contained in his articles in the *Columbia Lippincott Gazetteer.* The constituent units are listed as they existed in January, 1958.) Baku: Baku city and areas administratively subordinate thereto, and Sumgait city. Leningrad: city of Leningrad and areas administratively subordinate thereto; cities of Gatchina, Kronshtadt, and Lomonosov; rayons of Gatchina, Lomonosov, and Vsevolozhskiy. (Note: the areas subordinate to Leningrad proper in 1958 included the seven cities of Kolpino, Pavlovsk, Petrodvorets, Pushkin, Sestroretsk, Uritsk, and Zelenodolsk, and fifteen other localities.) Moscow (Moskva): city of Moskva and areas subordinate thereto; cities of Babushkin, Balashikha, Ivanteyevka, Khimki, Kuntsevo, Lyubertsy, Lyublino, Mytishchi, Perovo, Podolsk, Pushkino, Shchelkovo, and Tushino; rayons of Balashikha, Khimki, Krasnaya Polyana, Krasnogorsk, Kuntsevo, Lenino, Mytishchi, Podolsk, Shchelkovo, and Ukhtomskiy.

Sources: 1939 figures: *Izvestiya,* June 2, 1939; 1939 figure for Kopeysk from *Narodnoye khozyaystvo Chelyabinskoy oblasti* (Chelyabinsk, 1957; issued by the oblast statistical office). 1933 figure for Kiselevsk from the *Columbia Lippincott Gazetteer.* 1939 figure for Leningrad proper from *Narodnoye khozyaystvo goroda Leningrada* (Leningrad, 1957; issued by the city statistical office). Figures for cities annexed to U.S.S.R. since 1939 census: Sweden, Statistiska Centralbyrån, *Statistisk Årsbok, 1942* (Stockholm, 1942); Poland, Ministry of Information, *Concise Statistical Year-Book of Poland, September 1939–June 1941* (London, 1941); and Estonia, Bureau Central de Statistique, *Recueil Mensuel,* September 1939. 1956 figures: Tsentralnoye Statisticheskoye Upravleniye, *Narodnoye khozyaystvo SSSR v 1956 godu* (Moskva, 1957); *Narodnoye khozyaystvo SSSR* (Moskva, 1956); *Narodnoye khozyaystvo RSFSR* (Moskva, 1957). In addition to these, the M.A. delimitations made use of *Pravda,* January 13, 1954, and January 5, 1958; *Izvestiya,* December 25, 1954; *Moskovskaya Pravda,* December 24, 1952; *Leningradskaya Pravda,* December 26, 1952; RSFSR, Verkhovnyy Sovet, Prezidium, *RSFSR Administrativno-territorialnoye deleniye* (Moskva, 1955); Akademiia Nauk SSSR, Institut geografii, *Azerbaydzhanskaya SSR* (Moskva, 1957); the *Columbia Lippincott Gazetteer;* and data from various other sources, mainly of Soviet origin, compiled and supplied to IUR by Theodore Shabad.